# Business Grov

## How to Rapidly Create a Self-Sustaining Business

By
Dino Eliadis

117 N. Florida Avenue
Tarpon Springs, Florida 34689
Phone 727-487-5435• Fax 727-213-6234
Website: www.dinoeliadis.com
Email: info@dinoeliadis.com

Limits of Liability and Disclaimer of Warranty

## About This Book

This book is meant to help small business owners realize the life
independence and financial freedom they dreamed of when starting their
businesses. To accomplish this, it means getting your business to the
self-sustainability stage of the growth model. When you achieve this
level of business growth then you truly have choices: let your business
run itself "as is"; sell it when the market is ready; or scale it into a large
corporation.

If you are among the owners working longer and harder while getting
nowhere in your small business, then you need this book. Find out why
your business is stuck and your dreams are on hold, and how to get
unstuck and rapidly grow your business so you can have the choices that
a self-sustainable business offers.

# What People Say About This Book

"We didn't even know business self-sustainability was possible for a company of our size. After applying the growth model presented within this book to our business we, increased our monthly revenue by 156% in 16 months. With the profitability from this growth and by putting the right people and systems in place, we're discussing how we will spend our retirement from our business 12 months from now, and it will support us for the rest of our life without even having to sell the business!"

*– Jenn and Mike Rowe, owners, Generations Carpet Cleaning*

"The challenges confronting small business owners can often times seem insurmountable. As a small business owner himself, Dino Eliadis has confronted this reality for over a decade and his consulting clients have universally found peace of mind and prosperity through his guidance. I highly recommend this book for anyone running or thinking about starting a business."

*- Jim Lange, Infinity Consulting and Training*

"If you are thinking of starting a business, already successful and making money or thinking of your succession , exit or transition this book is a must read."

*– Michael C. Valdez, CLU, REBC, PA*

"Business Growth Simplified" would have been a great reference book for dozens of small business owners throughout Iraq and Afghanistan conflict areas we were assisting to enable growth and economic stability."

*- John Hamerlinck, Senior FDI Advisor, US Department of Defense*

"Dino Eliadis has discovered a method of taking the mystery out of growing your business and changes the way entrepreneurs operate. Small Business Growth Simplified is also a valuable road map for how economic development professionals can help the scalable companies in their communities grow and create job opportunities."

*- John Walsh, CEcD, Vice President, Pasco Economic Development Council, Inc.*

"Removing the complexity of many business growth theories, Dino introduces several business-owner characters the reader will follow as they work through real-life business growth issues together, making the content of this book relevant to business owners at any level of their growth curve. A "must read" if you are serious about the growth of your business."

*- Brian E. Powers, Executive Director, Chatham Technical Institute*

# Acknowledgements

This book is a testament to a lifetime of learning. Through it all there are too many people to thank. Listing them all would fill a book in itself. However I would like to thank everyone that has crossed my path both personally and professionally, you have influenced me in some way and made me who I am.

To all my clients over these many years, thank you for allowing me to share a part of your journey as it helped me hone my skills as an advisor. Without you I would not have had the confidence in the methods, strategies and tactics I share within this book.

Mom, to you I owe my "entrepreneur gene." You probably don't even realize that you passed on to me. To you Dad, thank you for your unrelenting drive toward achieving your goal. While I often complained about it to you, I realize that it gave me the strong work ethic and tenacity necessary to achieve a goal as lofty as the one I strive for every day.

To my first business coach and mentor Richard, I thank you for your wisdom and guidance in the early days. You taught me the importance of marketing and customer service. While you're no long here with us I know you look down and smile as you witness my accomplishments.

To Jim, my longest and most influential coach, mentor, business partner, friend, and "brother", thank you for all your faith in me. You saw my talent long before I ever did. Your undying commitment kept me going even when I wanted to give up. Entrepreneurship can be a lonely pursuit, but having you in my corner kept me going and taught me the value of believing in myself and never giving up on your dream.

To my book review team, thank you for your time and honesty. Your willingness to provide me the unvarnished truth has made this this book a better product, and in the process made me a better servant to the small business community that I serve.

Last, but most importantly, to my family Pam, Christopher, Timothy, and Matthew. Thank you for your patience and tolerance. I know the life that I have chosen often does not make me the easiest person to live with. But, I am grateful that you allow me to reach for my dream. My hope is that by sharing this part of my journey I have been an example to you and shown that through hard work and persistence toward your passion you can achieve your dreams. I love you with all of my heart!

# hiStory: Dino Eliadis

**Get Your Car Washed While You Wait!**

Car Washed............................................ $1.00

Vacuumed and Cleaned Inside............... $2.00

Cleaned and Waxed............................. $5.00

This is the sign that launched Dino's love for business and entrepreneurship. He was twelve and had his flash of genius came while watching parked cars. His mother ran an in-home beauty salon, and her customer's cars sat in the driveway while she washed, cut, dyed, and permed their hair. Dino saw a market opportunity and hung the sign on the salon bulletin board where customers, coming and going, would see his offer.

Dino made more money washing cars that summer than he did "working for the man" on his paper route. Dino was hooked on business! He credits his optimism, work ethic, and entrepreneurial gene to his family DNA, and his business successes to seizing opportunities and learning hard lessons.

Dino's grandparents emigrated from Greece in the early 1900s. His father, Bill, and grandfather, Constantine, were both steel workers before computers did the hard work. His mother, Billie, had her salon, and her father, Nick, was a shoemaker and owned his own business.

Medicine was Dino's original—and pricey—career choice. He enrolled in the Air Force ROTC to help pay for his education. And it was love of country, not medicine, that motivated Dino to complete college and graduate as an officer. While in the Air Force, he worked with missiles (trivia: the washout rate is higher than for pilots), in acquisitions, and in software engineering; managed projects with scary budgets and resources ($22 million and 1,600 people); and married and started a family with Pam.

His entrepreneurial fire was re-stoked, while earning his MBA in a swift eighteen months and a failed attempt with fellow airmen to purchase a local business. So after seven years, Dino left the military to build a business around what he knew best: software engineering consulting and aerospace. But eagerness and hard work are not substitutes for focusing on what truly matters in your business' stage of growth. Nearly exhausting their life savings, Dino and Pam filed for food stamps, welcomed a third child while on Medicaid, and Dino took side jobs. The business failed. Sound familiar?

Undaunted, his next business, Effective Information Solutions (EIS), focused on helping clients implement their CRM and sales automation systems. This time he paid attention to the factors that influenced his business growth at each stage. He was leading a client project that involved over 200 sales reps across 40-plus offices across the southeast when another company lured Dino to a corporate job that included managing projects for top-tier companies such as Nokia, Yellow Freight, and Clark Construction, as well as for mid-tier companies.

Dino next became a fulltime director at a large professional employer organization (PEO), which led to a chance reunion with a former client. This chance client encounter led to his next position as a director of sales and marketing for their new startup, mobile and wireless application development company.

On 9/11/2001, when other companies were closing, Dino started DE, Inc. to help businesses more rapidly move to the self-sustainability stage and beyond and always in alignment with owner values and goals.

Dino's life vision is to reduce the number of failed businesses in America by teaching each small business owner how to use their business as a vehicle for achieving *life independence and financial success*. Using SPARC (the Strategic Planning and Recovery Cycle) Business Growth Framework, Dino's clients learn to systematically standardize their business operation so it is repeatable, sustainable, and more importantly, scalable to a level necessary to make their life's vision a reality.

This book is Dino's way of making his knowledge more readily available to a larger number of small business owners. It makes DE, Inc. more systematic so it becomes repeatable, sustainable, and scalable to a level necessary to make Dino life's vision a reality.

# Table of Contents

# PART I
# Simplifying Business Growth for Your Business

# Chapter 1: Introduction

## Why business owners struggle growing their businesses

Small business owners tell me all the time, "I want to grow my business." So I ask them a simple question.

What kind of growth do you want; is it:

- top-line growth?
- bottom-line growth?
- market-share growth?
- some other type of growth?

The owner looks at me like a deer in the headlights or worse, and they say "Yes, all of that!"

And that's a dilemma, because to grow your business you need to pick one kind of growth to focus on, and have it be relevant to the maturity of your business!

Being unclear about the kind of growth they want is not the owner's fault! It's because all of the "so called" experts are providing marketing and sales advice and guidance. Those experts are not teaching them about the growth stages through which a business matures. That's because many of the experts don't understand the growth stages.

About the closest to stages of growth I ever hear from most trusted advisors is, "They're a stage one" or "They're a stage two" company. What the heck does that mean? I've never heard anyone give a solid definition and consistent characteristics of a stage one or a stage two company!

And herein lies another problem: The stages are not clearly defined growth paths for a business owner to follow. Instead, the stages are sales qualification terms as defined by a particular expert.

If you are a business owner, you talk to a dozen or more potential vendors or trusted advisors. They all are giving you a different definition of business growth. No wonder you feel lost and alone, nobody's helping you figure it out.

Why I wrote this book

Growing a business is simpler than you might think. Business growth is actually a well-defined and predictable process. Let me ask you, "If you knew what to do and when to do it, wouldn't growing your business be much simpler?"

The problem is nobody is teaching you the process! I have looked. Most organizations providing business owners with technical assistance are focused on teaching the functions of business which consist of marketing, sales, operations, and administration.

While tactics are important, which tactics and how you apply them change depending on your stage of growth. So as an owner, you may be taking the right actions at the wrong time or vice-versa. This will slow down your growth, or even damage your business.

This was the "ah ha moment" I had more than five years ago. It put me on a quest: to find a way to more effectively describe how tactics should be applied at different stages of a business's maturity.

As I began doing my research what I found is very interesting. There are hundreds of growth models out there. Heck, I was introduced to the business growth concept myself when getting my MBA way back in 1987. So if business growth isn't a new concept, why isn't it a more mainstream part of small business training?

There were all kinds of models out on the web. They come in all shapes and sizes. There are three stage, five stage, and even seven stage models. What is the right number of stages for a small business growth model?

As I read the characteristics of each stage, they all sort of hit the same areas. It was just that one author decided to draw their line one place and another decided to draw their line somewhere else. In some cases it was done for marketing reasons, to differentiate their model from the others. But that was not my intent. I just wanted to see if those who claim to be the experts agreed on how a small business matures. The surprising fact is that they all pretty much do.

I developed a business growth model as the basis for ALL DE, Inc.'s consulting and training and have used it since 2010 with great success. But I wanted to see more business owners apply it so that they could realize their dreams of personal independence and financial freedom.

## How to use this book to grow your business

As you read and begin to understand the business growth model, my hope is that you get clarity on what you need to focus on within yourself and your business to achieve your goals and dreams.

Think of the growth model as a *strategic roadmap* through which a business travels as it matures. The roadmap tells you what to do, and when to do it to get to the next level of maturity in your business. As a result you will now know which tactical actions are necessary. So you'll know what courses to take or what books to read, or what resources to apply to move yourself forward. Or you can hire the right advisor to help you or employees to do the work for you so you can get to the next level of success.

Most people learn better when they see a concept applied. So I have created three businesses and owners of these businesses to help better demonstrate how certain aspects of the growth model work.

But first you need a basic understanding of the growth model. So let's take a look'at the stages of growth and the factors that influence growth.

# Chapter 2: An Overview of the Business Growth Model

After reviewing dozens of resources, I settled on five or six that present some well thought out approaches to small business growth. I compiled all these models and approaches into a single comparative table for analysis.

The models had three, five, or seven stages; which left me wondering "What is the right number of stages for small business growth?" Reading the characteristics of each stage, I could see that the models all sort of hit the same points. It was just that the lines dividing the stages were drawn at different places.

## The 5 stages of business growth

The most significant approaches I found came from two Harvard Business Review articles: "The Five Stages of Small Business Growth" (Neil C. Churchill & Virginia L. Lewis, 1983) and "Evolution and Revolution as Organizations Grow" (Larry e. Greiner, 1972). These articles provided statistical research and had already been accepted by one of the premier business publications in the world. This was a good place to start.

From all of this complied data, I created a model by which small business owners could methodically grow their businesses to the point they could live out their dreams of personal independence and financial freedom.

Because this model is based on credible research, you can feel confident that by applying it in the proper sequence you will get the best results. The stages in the model are as follows:

1. Foundation

2. Survival

3. Self-Sustainability

4. Rapid Growth

5. Maturity

Another significant finding from the Churchill and Lewis paper was the fact that both *owner* and *company* factors are critical to a business's growth. This wasn't a new revelation to me. For decades, I have said that both leadership and management influences business performance. Let's look at the characteristics of the leadership and management factors that consistently influence business growth at every stage.

## The 8 factors you can influence to grow your business

To make the factors that influence business growth easier to understand, I've divided them into two groups: leadership growth and management growth.

### 4 Leadership growth factors

- **Owner Goals** — how the owner has decided to use the business as an asset that supports their personal dream.

- **Operational Skills** — how well the owner understands what the business does to generate revenue.

- **Managerial Abilities** — how well the owner understands how to direct the management growth factors towards achieving the owner's goals for the business.

- **Strategic Thinking** — how well the owner understands outside influences and applies the management growth factors to react to opportunities and threats to maximize return on the investment.

### 4 Management growth factors

- **Financial Assets** — the money-related resources necessary to achieve your business goals.

- **Personnel Resources** — the team necessary to achieve your business goals.

- **Systems** — the processes, procedures, and technologies used to achieve your business goals.

- **Business Assets** — those tangible and intangible things that a business both owns and that give value to the business, such as equipment, facilities, customer lists, intellectual property, and so on.

As you can see, there is much more at work here than just making sure the business is operating. The biggest thing that jumped out at me was that Churchill and Lewis had actually found a statistical correlation between business growth and an owner's abilities.

Before finding the Harvard Business Review articles, I had only observed the owner dynamic at work in client businesses. In fact, I felt the owner dynamic was a bigger influence on business growth than the management dynamic. Churchill and Lewis had just given me the third-party research I was looking for to state my case about how to grow my own business. Now I had it!

Read this book from the perspective of a business owner. You will find a number of new things that you hadn't considered before. If you then apply this newfound knowledge it will have a positive impact on your business growth.

This is the power of the leadership and management growth factors at work. Most often the reason that a business stagnates is because the owner has reached his or her limits of skills and knowledge. To keep growing, the owner needs to learn and apply the aspects of leadership and management growth that matter most for the next stage of business growth.

Now let's meet three business owners and their businesses. Although their names and businesses are fictitious, their situations are real. We'll use them as case studies of how you can move your own business through the business growth stages.

# Chapter 3: Meet the Companies and Their Owners

Our three business owners are at different stages in growing their businesses:

- Brandy Matthews has just started building her business, Matthews Training Tech, Inc.
  Her business is in Stage 1, Foundation.

- Chris and Ann Jordan have owned their business, Excellence Carpet Cleaning, Inc., for over 15 years.
  Their business is in Stage 2, Survival with a foot in the Foundation Stage.

- Mike Andrews bought his business 10 years ago and renamed it Andrews Mega Power, Inc.
  His business is in stage 2-3, Survival transitioning to the Self-Sustainability Stage.

## Matthews Training Tech, Inc. — Founder Brandy Matthews

*I'd like to introduce you to Brandy Matthews. Brandy, can you tell us a little bit about your background?*

Sure, I'd be happy to. I have a computer science degree from a reputable university and have worked for a number of different companies in several technical roles over the past fifteen years.

My last role was as the lead development engineer on a website project for a big customer service provider. Part of the project was to develop an online training system for the service provider's customers to use for customer support and to learn how to use the products that we represent.

*Can you tell us why you're thinking about starting up your own business?*

Well, the company chief technology officer (CTO) made the decision to use a third-party learning management system (LMS) as the training platform. It was my job to lead the integration and the implementation of the online training system part of the web site.

During this process, my team and I faced several different challenges. Many of the technical challenges were very complex and cost the project much more time and money than we originally expected. This put a lot of pressure on me and my team, but I learned a lot from the experience about training and LMSs during the process.

When the project was over, I took a well-deserved vacation with some friends. During dinner one evening, the project came up in a conversation. I shared a few of the challenges and how my team and I had overcome the challenges.

Two of my friends have their own businesses. They began asking more in-depth questions about if there was a better way to approach the problem. Based on my recent experience it was easy for me to immediately answer "Yes!"

As a result of that dinner conversation, I spent the rest of my vacation thinking about the project and doing what engineers do best - *coming up with solutions to problems.* My friends, helped me test different ideas and discussed ways that I might be able to turn them into a viable business. From there I started down my current path of really investigating how to start my business.

*That is pretty exciting! How did you begin the process of starting your business?*

When I got back from vacation I immediately began researching various local entrepreneurship programs. I contacted each of them to determine what they had to offer and began to lay them against my needs so that I could make the best decision for my situation.

*Did you quit your job and start any of the entrepreneurship programs yet?*

No, that's just not a realistic option at this point. I really don't have enough money to do that. Plus, I'm still not sure of exactly what I need to do to make money doing this!

*That's a good decision. I would have probably given you the same advice. So where are you at right now?*

During the day I continue to work at my engineering job. But I can't wait for work to be over and get home! This project is like a new toy on Christmas morning. I work on it from the time I get home until late into the night. I can't seem to get enough of this. Starting my own business has become my obsession!

I have decided on an entrepreneurship program and I have enrolled in their startup program. Classes have started, and I have really begun learning some business basics. I decided on a business name; and got the necessary legal documents filed to make it official. The name of my new business is *Matthews Training Tech, Inc.*

## Excellence Carpet Cleaning, Inc. — Founders Chris and Ann Jordan

*Meet Chris and Ann Jordan the owners of Excellence Carpet Cleaning. Hello! How are you two doing today?*

Things are going much better now that we've begun systematically approaching the growth of our business. We had no idea anything like this existed when we started our business. We've had the business for more than fifteen years, but the business has been up and down. Sometime things are great and for other things we are up late at night trying to figure out how we're going to pay the bills!

*Can you tell us a little bit about yourselves?*

Chris and I met in high school and got married after we graduated. We have two children, a girl seven years old and a son who's three. Chris grew up cleaning carpets. His family has been in the carpet cleaning business for decades. It is all he's known. Chris had already started ECC, the short name for our business, when we got married and we've been working it ever since.

*So Chris, you learned the business by working in it?*

Pretty much. Neither Ann nor I have any business education. We've learned everything we know on our own or with the help of friends or their accountant. We pretty much learn through the "school of hard knocks."

*Has the business provided for you and your family?*

I'd have to say yes, for the most part. We're not looking for a lot. We have a roof over our head; food on the table; and we're able to home school our kids and take a trip now and again. I don't think that we're really looking for much more than that out of our life. We do wish we could spend more time as a family though, while the kids are still little.

*Has it always been that way for you?*

N-o-o-o-o-o-o, during the recent economic downturn we got hit pretty hard. We had come to expect the business to provide for us at a certain level. We had sort of fallen into a comfort zone. Because we really didn't have a good way to monitor the business, we found ourselves in uncharted waters and struggling to make ends meet.

*What did you do?*

Scaled back personally. In the business we did what we have always done — worked hard and provided exceptional value and rode out the storm. We had to sell the house and move into a rental property. Lost our boat and really were worried how bad things could get. Our faith help us get through it all, but it definitely made us really think about making a change.

*What kind of change were you thinking about making?*

We thought about scrapping it all, moving, and just starting new. It was at this point that Chris met a business coach by happenstance at a networking event. It was through this chance encounter that we learned about the concept of business self-sustainability. It was the answer to the question we'd been asking for a long time. After hearing about business self-sustainability we knew it was how we wanted to build ECC so it could stand on its own and provide for our family and the families of the people that we employ.

## Andrews Mega Power, Inc. - Founder/CEO Mike Andrews

*I'd like to introduce you to Mike Andrews owner of Andrews Mega Power. Tell us how you've been able to grow Mega Power into a multi-million dollar business?*

I'd be happy to share my story with you. I began my career out of college as a sales rep for a manufacturing distribution company. I was a top-tier sales rep from the start, consistently blowing my quota out of the water every quarter. I never missed a year making the president's club.

During my time at the distributor, I caught the eye of the owner of Mega Power. Bill was an older gentleman who was ready to retire. He made me an offer to come on-board and run the sales department. While I was in charge of sales I grew top-line revenue by 10–22% every year.

After about three years, Bill decided he was ready to retire and offered me the business. We structured a deal that allowed me to purchase the business over the next ten years. As a result, I was able to acquire the business and now I own it outright.

*Sounds like you've done alright for yourself?*

I think so. I've been in business for nearly two decades and have consistently had strong net profit, year after year. I serve on several boards around town. And I seem to be the "go to" person for many organizations around town when they want someone to speak about business success to small business owners in the area. I've been recognized by countless organizations both locally and nationally within our industry. So. I would say I am pretty successful.

*Would you be willing to share a little bit more about you on a more personal note?*

Sure, that part of me is even more important to me than my business. I have been married to my wife, Cathy, for nearly 30 years. We live out of town on the lake as we like to play on the weekends, especially with our three children and their families.

The kids grown, done with college, and out of the house. Two of our kids are married and have children of their own. Our daughter and her husband live here locally, but our son and his wife live out of state.

*So it sounds like things are settling into a good rhythm for you. Have you started thinking about retiring and exiting your business?*

Cathy and I want to spend more time with our grandchild. She's been pressuring me to fix the business or get rid of it! She is ready to enjoy our grandchildren and all the great things that our success has given to us. But it seems that I can't leave the business for any length of time. Some crisis always seems to spring up and need my attention.

*Have you ever tried fixing it?*

Yeah, I have had a dozen consultants and business coaches in here over the years come in and try to "fix the business." I don't know what the problem is. Nobody seems to want to step up and take charge!

# Chapter 4: Exploring the 5 Stages of Business Growth

Now that you have a general outline of the growth model and its components, let's take a deeper dive. To use the model to get results, it is important for you, as an owner, to understand it in more detail.

First, I'll take you through the stages. The major thing to understand about the stages is that each has *one*, and *only one* goal. When you achieve that goal you move to the next stage of growth.

It's that easy! Achieve the goal and your business grows.

So what makes it so hard? That's easy to answer; it's because nobody has shown you the model or told you "this is all you need to concern yourself with at this stage of your business's growth."

Now do you see why I said this subject is so important? You're getting bombarded by business experts telling you, "You need social media; you need accounting; you need legal help; you need equipment; you need a loan; you need ___fill in the blank___. But which do you really need? The answer is this: use the model described in this book, you can confidently select the right help based on what you really need to accomplish at your particular stage of business growth.

Now, let's take a closer look at each of the five stages and their primary focus.

## Stage 1: Foundation

*Goal: Get monthly cash flow to the point of consistent breakeven.*

You might think that the foundation stage is the same as the startup stage of a company. But in fact, there are many businesses that have existed for years and still cannot break even month to month.

Businesses in the foundation stage need better owner leadership and management that is focused on creating consistent monthly cash flow. In a later section, you'll learn about strategies to help you get out of the foundation stage and move on to making real profits.

## Stage 2: Survival

*Goal: Consistently achieve owner-established profit requirement.*

The shift at this stage is to move from breaking even every month to profitability. As an owner, you have invested time, money, and hard work into your business. Now that you are breaking even, you need to begin getting a return on investment (ROI).

This means going beyond just making enough to keep the doors open. You must begin expanding the systems created in the foundation stage to consistently meet a profit requirement you have set for your business. Notice it's a profit requirement and not a goal. That's because to become independent and financially free, there's a certain amount of income that the business must generate for you.

Your level of business knowledge needs to increase, too, or your business will begin to stagnate. In a later section you'll see why so many business owners get stuck here in the survival stage. It's what I call "nowhere land."

## Stage 3: Self-Sustainability

*Goal Path A. Sustain the business's success created to this point.*

*or*

*Goal Path B. Rapidly grow the business to a large corporation.*

When you achieve the self-sustainability stage, your business consistently generates a profit without you, and you have the independence and financial freedom to choose your next goal.

Sustaining success means you are choosing to let your business run itself in a way that keeps it the same size until you are ready to act on your business succession or exit plan. Rapidly growing means you are choosing to grow your business into a large corporation with the help of an executive team.

But beware: self-sustainability is where many owners get mired between self-sustainability and survival. In fact, many owners think they are in self-sustainability when they are actually still in survival. So how do you know if you are firmly in self-sustainability? Take the self-sustainability litmus test.

*Litmus test: Does the business consistently generate*
*profit without owner intervention?*

If your answer is "Yes," then your business is self-sustainable and has real value because it is running itself. If your answer is "No," then your business is stuck in survival because it relies on you, the owner, to consistently generate profit. And being stuck in survival has consequences: you still have a job; and it will be difficult, if not impossible to do what you really want to do, whether it's to stay the same size until you act on your succession or exit plan or to move to rapid growth.

## Stage 4: Rapid Growth

*Goal: Assure that growth does not outpace assets,*
*resources, and systems.*

The rapid growth stage is based on an owner's decision in the self-sustainability stage to grow the business into a large corporation (as opposed to disengaging and keeping the business the same size).

Self-sabotage can be a problem in the rapid growth stage as many business owners started their business to get *out* of the corporate grind. Being part of the corporate grind means that you are a cog in a self-sustaining system because you are serving in some kind of operational role. It stands to reason that if you continue in an operational role in your business, then you've created your own corporate grind and your own place as a cog.

In the rapid growth stage, large sums of capital are needed as the business takes on more and more customers and therefore requires more people, equipment, and materials. The resources needed to service these new customers seems ever expanding. Properly executed, it is in this stage that a small business becomes a big company. If not managed properly, this stage can be the death of a company. Yet many business owners resist and sabotage their rapid growth efforts by refusing to give up their operational roles.

You can combat this problem using DE, Inc.'s Personal and Business Goal Assessment. You can find this tool on our website www.dinoeliadis.com.

## Stage 5: Maturity

*Goal: To diversify the company by offering related products or services to existing customers or by entering new markets.*

Once it achieves rapid growth, a business moves into maturity. The all-too-typical characteristics of businesses in the maturity stage are that they are big and lethargic. The business has again reached a plateau. It has saturated its market or outgrown its management team's ability to manage the business's growth. Businesses in the maturity stage often cannot react to major shifts in the market and die as a result. But well managed businesses in this stage begin to diversify in ways that allow the company to continue to grow.

Work in the maturity stage is accomplished by moving into other markets or finding related products for the existing customer base. These other markets or products are really other entities in earlier stages of the growth model. So you may see different parts of the business begin working at different stages of the growth model.

For example, you might look at new product development as a strategy here. The new product is just another application of the foundation stage. So the growth model can operate at various levels within a business that offers several products or serves more than one market.

## Business growth stage illusions

At first glance you might think that Brandy is firmly in the foundation stage; Chris and Ann are firmly in the survival stage; and Mike is firmly in the self-sustainability stage. However, you would be incorrect.

You need to take more into consideration than just a cursory look at the business. Later in this book, an assessment tool will be introduced to help you with this process. For now, let's just look at the goal of each stage and where each of our companies stacks up to the goal.

First, Matthews Training Tech is clearly in the foundation stage, but not firmly. The goal of the foundation stage is to get monthly cash flow to the point of consistent breakeven. But Brandy has not yet started collecting revenue. This means her business is not consistently breaking even each month which is the primary goal of the foundation stage.

Next let's look at Excellence Carpet Cleaning. Chris and Ann have done alright through the years, but during a downturn they nearly went out of business. This means that they were more than breaking even every month and then they weren't. This would indicate that they are profitable during good times and have trouble when times are bad.

Chris and Ann have a foot in the survival stage but cannot seem to firmly keep it there. The goal of the survival stage is to consistently achieve an owner-established profit requirement. We will need to look closer at their situation. There are probably some specific strategies they can use to make sure they stay solidly in the survival stage. Then they can begin working on the self-sustainability stage.

Finally, let's look at Mega Power which appears by most people's definition to be a truly self-sustainability stage company. But is it really by the definition presented here?

The goal of self-sustainability is to run the business without the owner so that the business can move to **either** rapid growth or stay firmly planted in the self-sustainability stage.

Mega Power is turning a hefty profit and has been doing so for many years. This is business success, isn't it? Well, not really because Mike and his wife want to take more vacations and time for themselves and they cannot. The business is an albatross around Mike's neck. He is chained to the business, and that is not success.

Mike needs to wean himself off his dependence on his business. This is easier said than done. It appears at times that Mike is dependent on the business too! This is a challenge for many owners and should prove to be an interesting plot as we progress further in his story.

## To know your stage and goal, know your factors

So now we have several big ideas about what it takes to grow your business. You know it happens in five stages and that each stage has just one goal. You also know that if you want to achieve the goal for a particular stage, then you have to both lead and manage, which you do by paying attention to eight growth factors.

Having looked at the five stages of growth has probably given you a much better perspective on how a business matures. Also, doesn't having a defined goal make things much easier?

But how do you know which stage you are in so that you can focus on the right goal? Well, when you first saw the list of growth factors you probably were drawn to one or more of them. It was probably because, as an owner, you know this is an area where you are weak. Guess what? That's probably why your business isn't growing as fast you want!

Stop right now and take a moment to honestly consider your weak points. Go ahead; mark the list below. What do most need to improve in your leadership and management areas?

### Leadership (Self and Team) - Owner Factors

- Owner Goals
- Operational Skills
- Managerial Abilities
- Strategic Thinking

### Management - Company Factors

- Financial Assets
- Personnel Resources
- Systems
- Business Assets

Let's see how the owners you met earlier feel they fall within the growth model, now that they've learned about the eight factors that influence business growth.

## Chapter 5: Leadership Factors Influencing Business Growth

The leadership factors relate to the leadership knowledge and skills of the owner. After more than two decades of helping small business owners, I believe that the leadership factors are more important to business growth than the management factors. Let me show you what I mean.

Small business owners tend to blame their growth issues on not having good financial reporting, or not having good marketing, or not having some other thing or things. I thwart these conversations early by asking "You're the owner, so you're in charge — right? If your business doesn't have these things, why not?"

This usually interrupts their pattern of thought. Now we can begin having a real discussion about the things that they don't understand about business and leadership so their learning process can begin.

The four leadership factors that small business owners need to master are:

- Owner Goals
- Operational Skills
- Managerial Abilities
- Strategic Thinking

### Owner goals

While this factor is titled as "owner goals" it is really much more than that. After consulting with business owners for more than two decades, I have found one of the biggest challenges that they face is *themselves!*

This was an "ah ha moment" for me a long time ago, and the inspiration for the DE, Inc. tagline:

*Personal Growth, Business Leadership, Life Success*

The tagline outlines the order in which success is achieved. When you try to do it out of order, the results are usually short-lived, are less than you wanted, or end in disaster.

Think about the other business owners you know. Which ones are truly happy and which ones seem to struggle? If you asked the ones struggling about personal things in their lives, you will usually find some type of turmoil. Or, even worse, they won't talk about it at all! In this case, there is probably something deep and too painful or embarrassing to share.

What pain and embarrassment are holding you back? You need to know and overcome that before you'll ever achieve true business success.

Now ask business owners who *have* their act together and are happy beyond belief about their personal lives. You will find that their success with their family, friends, and personal goals seems to bleed over into their business success. Their life is completely aligned.

Until you really know what you want from your life you can never really set your business up properly to give it to you. So the most important thing you can do when starting a new business is ask yourself two questions:

1. Why am I doing this?

2. What hole in my life does this business help me this fill?

Without a good answer to those questions, you will one day wake up — as many of our first-time clients do — and ask yourself, "Why the heck did I ever start this business?" Once we help them get clarity on their life's purpose, their business takes on a whole new perspective and growth becomes a natural outcome!

Let's look at each of the case study businesses. Have their goals been helping them or hindering them?

## Our owners' goals

*Brandy, why did you decide to pursue your new business venture?*

I think that there is a better solution to the problem that we ran into on my most recent project at work. As an engineer, solving problems, is what I love doing.

*But is this a good enough reason for you to start your own business? There is a lot more that comes with business ownership — sales, marketing, making payroll, paying bills, collecting revenue from customers. The list is almost endless. Having a business means doing all these things — in addition to your providing your service or product — and more.*

*I see this situation with startups all the time. The owners get caught in the glitz and glamor, but they never see the reality. Having your own business is more work than most people are really willing to do. Once they get into business they're forced to do whatever it takes to pay the* bills. And then the business becomes a miserable job instead of a path to independence and financial freedom. Have you thought about this?

Well, I think I have. This is one of the reasons that I signed up with the entrepreneurship program at our local business incubator. I am learning everything that I need to do. So far I haven't seen anything that would make me say "I won't do that." So signing up for the incubator program has been a great investment in allowing me to evaluate whether I should start and business or not.

*Chris and Ann, how about you? What is your "why"?*

Good question! We have thought about this a lot lately. Everything always comes back to our kids and our family. The business is just a means to that end for us. Because we've never really experienced anything else, we don't know what other options we have, so we just keep doing what we're doing. It puts food on the table and keeps a roof over our head.

*Your situation is one that I hear from many business owners I meet. You approach your business as an income source and not like an asset that should produce income on its own for you. As a result, you keep working until something rocks the boat and gets your attention. This is usually gets you to do some soul-searching and it's from this soul-searching that change happens.*

*What was the recent event that compelled you to do some soul searching?*

The recent downturn in the economy hit us pretty hard. Then Chris's dad, who has a bigger cleaning business in South Carolina, asked us to come and run one of his service areas. We've never really lived anywhere else so it sounds like a great adventure. The problem is what do we do with our business here? Then we met you by happenstance. This whole idea of business self-sustainability gives us what we want and more. So this is the path we've decided to commit ourselves and our business to.

*Mike you've already reached your goal — right?*

You might think so, but I don't have the independence that I want. I'm still tied to the business!

The added pressure from Cathy to begin our retirement and spending more time with the grandchildren is the motivation that has me thinking. When I look back at why I built this business it was all for them! Now, it has become a ball and chain, and keeps me from doing what I want with my family.

*Wow, I can see how that really got you thinking. What is the one thing that keeps you up at night?*

That the business could drive a wedge between me and Cathy! We've been together for more than 30 years. She means the world to me and to have the business be what tears us apart wakes me in a cold sweat!

*That's a pretty scary nightmare. But the fact that you recognize it means you can do something about it. I have seen my share of this before. I have had to become a marriage counselor more than once over the years.*

*Could Cathy do some of these things on her own?*

Sure, she's not tied to the business, and she will not hesitate to visit the grandchildren on her own. But this is not the retirement we planned. Running the business like I always have is just a stop gap for now. I really have to do something different so I can get back to enjoying my business and my family.

I like what I've heard with this concept of business self-sustainability. The business is successful, our profits prove it. I just haven't been able to figure out how to make self-sustainable, and neither have any of the other consultants that I've brought in before. They talked about it, but they never provided me with the "how to" to make it happen. I'm hoping you'll be able to show me how to do it.

*That's the idea Mike. One thing that I can tell you, is that you have the right motivation to achieve self-sustainability. And, the fact that you've admitted you don't know how to do it is your first step toward making it happen. Many owners won't admit they have a problem or won't take ownership of it. No consultant can help someone who doesn't think they have a problem or who won't commit to solving it.*

## Operational skills

By "operational skills" we mean how well the owner understands what the business does to generate revenue. Operational skills are a leadership factor and often a business owner's biggest strength and their main reason for starting their own business. They were working for someone else and felt they could do a better job themselves.

The problem with their rationale is that owning a business takes more than just operational skills. A business has many functions other than "operations" that directly or indirectly help generate revenue; and when these functions are not done properly you can bet that the business owner suffers many headaches and sleepless nights.

Another problem I have observed is that most business owners are good in one of two operational areas:

- technical ability, or
- selling ability

That is, either they are one of the best at delivering their service or product, or they can sell the heck out of just about anything. The problem is a successful business needs both technical ability and selling ability as part of their operational skill set! So you have to learn how to do the thing you struggle with or you need to hire someone who can do it for you.

But even if you hire someone to do the technical work or selling work, you will still need to acquire some minimum level of skill yourself. If you abdicate instead of delegating the function, your business will eventually be stolen out from under you or you will never get the results that you want and reach the level of success that you want.

So you still need to learn the other operational aspects of business where you struggle even if you don't do it yourself. This is one of the reasons small business owners struggle. They don't want to do the work that they aren't good at or think they won't be good at. As a result, the business only grows to the lowest level of the owner's competence in whatever area that competence might be and the business's growth stops right there.

## Our owners' operational skills

*Give me your assessment of your operational skills, Mike.*

Well, I guess it depends on what you equate to operational ability. I was the top sales rep for my original employer, the manufacturing distributor. I like to think that I can sell like nobody's business; and I did that for Mega Power as well in the beginning. But now I understand being able to sell doesn't mean I can manage a full-blown sales team and run a company too.

I solved that problem by hiring a VP of sales. Don't get me wrong, I still love selling! I'll do deals whenever I get the opportunity. However, most of the sales for the company are done by the sales team.

*Chris and Ann what about you? How would you rate your operational skills?*

Remember I grew up in the carpet cleaning business. I do a great job and our customers tell us that every day.

I think where I struggle is finding others to do what I do. My question is how do I train others to the level necessary to delegate what I do to others? This has always be a challenge for us.

*Chris, this is a great question! We will take a look at how you do that a little later. Right now I want to ask Brandy the same question, how would you rate your operational skills?*

I am a technical expert. I'd put my technical skills up against anybody else's technical competence.

I also like to think I have adequate leadership skills, having managed lots of development projects over my years in the corporate world.

*I don't think operations will be a problem for you, Brandy. But can you learn what's needed on the management and sales side to do that part of the business too?*

Funny you should bring that up. At first this was what kept me up at night thinking about it. But as I have learned more about what it means to sell services and manage a business, I can look back and see where I used operational skills in my project work. Guess what, this doesn't keep me up at night anymore!

*A good observation, Brandy. I would agree with your assessment. You do have the operational skills, and you just need to learn to apply them to your business and not just projects.*

## Managerial abilities

As I mentioned previously, many business owners get started because they were good at their jobs. That doesn't make you a business owner. You have to know how to run a business.

A common problem is that people take the "business-like" skills they have in running their household, such as paying the bills, and mistake this for managing their business!

A business is an entirely different animal! While there are aspects to running a home that can be transferred to your business, you cannot stop there; because if you do, then your business growth will also stop. This happens because knowing how to run the household does not give you sufficient experience in handling the volume of what needs to be done in the business.

You need to learn how to systematically operate your business. DE, Inc.'s Tuning Your Revenue Engine management model can assist. Find this tool on our website www.dinoeliadis.com/business-growth/small-business-management.

## Our owners' managerial abilities

*Brandy how do you think that you stack up in the management area?*

Like I said before, I thought I was lacking in the management area. However, I now see the parallels between management of a business and project management; both require many of the same skill sets. The skills are not all the same and there will be others I need to learn. But I feel like I am closer that I thought at first.

*What about you two, Chris and Ann?*

We both have struggled here. We look for advice from our trusted advisors like business owner friends, our tax accountant, and such. However, their advice has not been enough to really help us manage and grow our business. Honestly, I think Chris and I manage the business from our business checkbook. We have minimal monthly financial data. I do a pretty good job managing our accounts receivable but that's because I get scared when I see the checkbook gets below a certain level.

On the sales and marketing front we don't have anything. We get calls here and there from our website, but not enough to really grow the business. We don't track how many orders we get when our commercial clients call. Our marketing is nearly non-existent. We only seem to focus on it when we are in a panic because we've lost a client and see that our revenue won't cover our bills.

*I would title your situation in one word — survival!*

*What about you, Mike how would you rate your managerial abilities?*

I'm not formally trained in business. I picked up what I needed through mentors and CEO forums that I attended over the years. I learned what I needed to grow the business to its current size. I know my key metrics and monitor those metrics regularly. I have the pulse of Mega Power day-to-day and manage the business accordingly. I get asked by local business organizations all the time to come in and talk about how I manage and run the company. I don't think I have any issues that are management related.

*I would say that you're probably right, but let's not make that judgment until we get a full picture of your situation.*

Ok, I think that's fair. Besides, I am hoping this is what I need to help me get out from under Mega Power so that Cathy and I can retire!

## Strategic thinking

The debate over strategy versus tactics rages on and on. It is an important topic, and you'll see why in a moment. However, if you ask any trusted advisor you'll find that everyone has a little different opinion regarding strategy and tactics. Usually their opinion is based on their perspective. First you need to understand is that there are strategies for growing your business and strategies for managing finances, production, personnel, and every other function in your business. As a result, your business growth strategy could become complicated. But it doesn't have to be.

To keep it simple — whether it's just you or you and your advisors — approach strategic thinking by asking these questions in this order:

1. What is my overarching personal goal?
2. What is the goal for the stage of growth my business is in?
3. Where am I stuck in achieving that goal?
4. What strategies will help me get unstuck?
5. For the strategies I choose, what are the tactics?

Here is a simple example you can use to see the difference between strategy and tactics: the "build versus buy versus do nothing" strategy.

This strategy can be applied to nearly anything you do in your business! Think about any aspect of your business:

- You can build it — do it in-house using the skills your skills or your employees' skills.
- You can buy — outsource it; services exist to help you with *anything* in your business.
- Do nothing — ignore it. This is where many small business owners get into problems; they do things they should not be doing at all. If it doesn't add value or revenue then *don't do it*!

Once you have selected the strategy it's time to apply the tactics. Tactics are the actions you take to execute the strategy you selected. This is doing and managing the work. Think about that. If you decide to do it in-house your actions are very different than if you plan to outsource it. The resources you need will most likely also change.

Now isn't that easier than you thought? The reason many "so called experts" complicate strategy is because they're trying to rationalize why they need to charge you so much money.

In some cases a high price is warranted. When the tactics associated with a strategy are complex, like in highly regulated industries, then obviously there is a reason to charge a lot and to expect to pay a lot.

Additionally, in order to select the right strategy you have to conduct a lot of analysis. This usually takes the form of a cost/benefit analysis. But, you also want to compare the pros and cons of each strategy to achieving your goal and objectives. There is more than just money involved. We've all seen rich people that are miserable with life. This is because they didn't align their life's goals with the money. As a result they didn't get the best results or return on investment.

So strategy isn't just "shooting from the hip." Improving your strategic thinking means rolling up your sleeves and really looking at the details of each strategic approach for your situation *before* you make a decision. Are you up to the challenge? The success of your business is at stake here.

Often getting better at strategy is just learning to be more disciplined at digging into the details. As you begin having more information on which to make your decisions, the right choice becomes clearer, and your decisions become better as a result. Sometimes that's all it takes to grow your business — making better decisions!

## Our owners' strategic thinking

*Let's start with you, Mike. How would you rate your strategic thinking?*

I like to think that I am an excellent strategist. This is one of the reasons that I get asked to participate in so many community projects and boards. I know how to ask the right questions and challenge the unchallenged areas to find the hidden gotchas. I don't think I have a problem with my strategic thinking. But again I don't want to make that assumption and get burned by my ego.

*Mike, you seem to be finding humility; this is a crucial first step. Growing a business involves putting egos aside.*

*Chris and Ann how do you rate your strategic thinking?*

We struggle here a little bit. We tend to do the first thing that comes to mind. When we have an idea we don't think it all the way through.

*So you don't look at all your options and do a cost/benefit analysis of each approach?*

No, and we know this a problem. We have been burned more than a few times when trying new things. It's made us a little gun shy. We are hesitant — or even terrified — about trying something new. We're tired of getting burned.

*I can understand that. How do you feel like this is affecting you and your business?*

We are frozen about doing anything at all. I think this is why we were looking to move and start over before we met you. We feel like we're in a state of perpetual mediocrity, just following the status quo day-to-day. It's made us more than a little disenchanted with our business. We're looking for a way out and a new opportunity wherever we can find one.

*You have to be careful with this. If you don't learn to apply strategic thinking, then even a completely new endeavor could just be another disaster waiting to happen.*

*How about you Brandy, what's the quality of your strategic thinking?*

Coming from the corporate world, I am familiar with the difference between strategy and tactics. But I'm not familiar with all the strategies necessary to have and grow my own business.

*I don't know if this will be a problem. You seem to be taking the right steps. You sought out help via entrepreneurship programs in the area. Most entrepreneurship programs provide a good introduction to the many different strategies necessary to start a business. If there is anything that is usually lacking in these programs, then it's a lack of an overall methodology of how to tie all of the growth strategies into a single and comprehensive business strategy and operational plan.*

## Checking in with our owners

*Brandy, based on the leadership and management factors that influence growth, where would you say that you and your business would be classified?*

If I understand this model correctly, then I'd say I fall in the foundation stage!

*Why do think your business is in the foundation stage?*

Well for one thing, I haven't started making money. So I haven't achieved breakeven yet. Heck, I haven't even figured out what my breakeven point is! We're learning about it in my entrepreneurship class.

Also, I don't understand some of the growth factors. What do you mean when you talk about strategic thinking? I do know how to manage a project, but I don't have any experience managing a business. And I confess, in college, the business management courses were painful. It's programming and the joy of seeing it solve problems that I really love.

*How about you, Ann and Chris, at what stage do you think that you and your company are?*

Well, we have done OK to this point. We have begun seeing how much we have already learned on our own. But the problem is we don't really know how to use it all. Besides, a lot of this stuff just doesn't seem to apply to our business. This stuff is just for big companies, right?

*Well, that's not really the case. I think as we dig deeper that you'll begin seeing how applying the growth factors can help your business stay profitable even in a down economy. In other words, when you apply the growth factors, then your business goes where you want it to go. And when you don't apply the growth factors, then your business sort of goes wherever the economy is going.*

*What about you Mike. Where is the growth stage of your business?*

I know my stuff! I don't see anything here that I haven't heard before. In fact, we apply all of this stuff within Mega Power!

*I don't know if I agree, Mike. Are you able, right now, to step away from your business and have it continue to run without you? This is what business self-sustainability is all about, stepping away from the business and it keeps on producing as if you were there.*

*The problem you all have is similar to what most business owners — your blind spots. If you can't identify and master the most important growth factors for your growth stage, then it's a good bet that your business isn't growing because you are spending effort and resources in the wrong areas. This is why it is important to understand how a business matures before you spend time and money learning tactics. Learn only what you need based on where you and your business are along the growth model and you can accelerate your business growth.*

# Chapter 6: Management Factors Influencing Business Growth

The management growth factors are the things you normally think of when you think of running a business and of growing it.

Management is also *not* what small business owners want to talk about. Small business owners want to talk about business functions: marketing, sales, production, accounting, finance, customer service, and so on.

Now look at the four management growth factors:

- Financial assets
- Personnel resources
- Systems
- Business assets

While business functions are important, each one must have the four management growth factors applied to it or the business function cannot operate optimally and you will not be able to accomplish your goals.

## Financial assets

Financial assets are everything money related. As you know, money is a huge factor in everything you do personally or professionally. This means the better steward of money you become, the more effective you will be in managing larger sums of money; and managing increasingly larger sums of money is key to business growth.

You may be surprised to find that your CPA may not be your best teacher here. Many CPAs focus on taxes which is only one facet of financial management. If this is the case with your CPA (or whoever does your taxes), then be aware that their financial advice and guidance may be one dimensional. Tax management is only a very small piece of the financial puzzle.

What you really need as a business owner is *managerial accounting*. What's the different you ask? A *great* question! Managerial accounting is setting up your books so that you can monitor what's *actually* happening in your business, so that you can determine the results based on your business's day-to-day activity. That is, you do this amount of marketing, selling, and delivery, and the result is this amount of revenue, this percent cost of goods, this percent of expenses, and this percent of net profit.

I can't teach you everything you need to know about financial management here. In fact, I am not the best person to do it. My tactical expertise is not finance and accounting. Your best bet here is to find a good bookkeeping service or a CPA who can help. Make sure that in addition to being an expert with accounting software, the person you hire has plenty of financial management and accounting experience with small and medium-size businesses. A small business has a completely different set of financial challenges than a big corporation. Once you reach the self-sustainability stage and set a goal to move into the rapid growth stage, then you *might* need a CPA who specializes in working with big businesses.

This brings up another good point. Merely using QuickBooks or any other accounting software package *is not* financial management. That is like saying because you bought a box of tools you're now a mechanic. Most financial management experts will tell you the biggest challenge that they see is business owners who lack an understanding of basic accounting principles. If you, as a business owner, don't understand basic accounting then the software will not help. If you've never had — or it's been a long time since you had — a formal accounting class, then you need to take a class or read a book on basic accounting.

## Our owners' understanding of financial assets

*OK, business owners; let's talk money. Let's start with Mega Power. Mike tell us about how you manage your financial assets for Mega Power.*

I am all over my financials! First, I have set up a dashboard report that helps me monitor financial health of the company on a regular basis. I get reports daily, weekly, and monthly on my key performance indicators, also known as KPIs. I don't make a decision without looking at these reports first.

*Wow, that's pretty impressive. Do you feel like these tools have helped you in growing your business?*

It's hard to get to Mega Power's level of profitability and not have learned some financial skills along the way.

*I would agree with you there, Mike. Let's ask a similar question to you Chris and Ann. How are your financial asset management skills?*

We have not really had any real financial training. It has never really been a priority, and when it is then it's too late. Our financial management consists of, "if there is money in the bank then everything is OK."

But after hearing Mike's answer, we see that we really need to make this a higher priority. There has to be more to managing our financial assets than just managing our checkbook.

*I agree. Cash is not your only financial asset, and managing cash from your checkbook is not financial management. I am sure you both will agree that there is far more going on in your business than just your bank account. You have bills, daily expenses, and accounts payable that don't show up right away.*

Boy, when you put it that way, you're right; we're missing a lot of other financial assets that we have right at our fingertips. If we subtract what we owe from our bank balance that gives us a different perspective all together.

I haven't ever thought about our outstanding invoices in that way either. When money gets tight then I just look at what's coming in that week and pay the bills we can based on that. But it —financial management — is not a formal thing that we do regularly like Mike does.

*What if you took all those invoices that you have out there that have not yet been collected and add that amount back into your bank balance? Does that raise your comfort level a little?*

Well sure. That's usually more than we have in the bank account at any one time!

*I am over-simplifying things here, but it doesn't have to be complicated to be useful. I believe that this is one reason so many small business owners shy away from learning accounting. Most accounting professionals try to teach you full-blown accounting, which is complicated and overkill for what you need as a business owner to manage your business.*

*My philosophy is this: learn the basic principles and hire a professional to advise you when you need it. If you grow the business big enough you'll have to hire a controller or CFO. By then you might need to know more — and in fact, you'll probably have learned more — than just basic accounting, but you still won't need to be an accounting expert yourself.*

*What about you, Brandy? While you don't have money coming in right now, you are spending it. What are your financial management skills?*

I have some skills because as a project manager I have to budget and monitor costs as my team is executing the project. I think I just need to understand how to apply financial skills to a much bigger and complex project: my business.

*I think you've hit the nail on the head. I come from the project management world, too, and have always approached business from a project management perspective. Most people have managed a project at one time or another in their life. When I make the correlation it seems to ease people's minds about what's involved in financial management. If you learn how to manage projects then you can learn to manage a business. Sometimes a little confidence is all you need to succeed. So run with what you're thinking, Brandy. You'll be just fine.*

Thanks, that gives me a more confidence about getting my business rolling!

## Personnel resources

Personnel resources refer to everything people-oriented in your business. This doesn't just mean human resources (HR). HR is the administrative side of personnel resources, but there is far more than just that required.

If you've hired people in your business you know all the work that goes into getting a new employee up to speed and producing revenue for your business. That is another dimension on the personnel factor.

It also takes into account how you deploy your people. Are you giving them work that helps you produce the most revenue possible? That's right; if your people aren't helping you produce revenue, either directly in production or in support in administrative roles, then why do you have them?

This is a key point. All the resources are *assets* of your business. And, what is the purpose of assets in a business? It is to *generate revenue!*

## Our owners' understanding of personnel resources

*Brandy, tell us about your experience in hiring and firing.*

I've built teams for my projects. I like to think that I know how to motivate people toward a goal. However, most of what I have needed for projects was supplied by the companies that I worked for. So I have no experience in finding talent and all the legal mumbo jumbo that goes with all that. There was always an HR director helping with that stuff.

*Good that you see that potential challenge. You might want to think about finding an HR consultant or someone who does staffing to help you when you get to that point.*

*What about ECC? Ann and Chris what's your experience with hiring and firing employees?*

We have had mixed success with hiring. We have had great employees and bad ones.

There have been times when we decided that we wanted to grow the business and make a hire. But then later, the sales weren't there to support the hire. We felt bad about having to fire someone and kept them on longer than we should have. As a result, we put a financial burden on the business and our family.

So now we are more than a little fearful of hiring for growth. But we know we have to if we want to grow the business; hiring more employees is a must. How do we get past our fear of hiring employees so we can grow the business?

*Good question that we will talk about later. But I want to point out something else to you here. You are aware that this is a fear that you have to conquer, and that's good, as it's the first step in moving forward!*

*Mike what about you? I am sure you've hired and fired your share of people over the years?*

Yeah, I lost count a long time ago. In our company this is second nature. Heck, Mega Power even has an HR director! So we have this is well under control.

*Do you? Not to be direct, but what about hiring your replacement? Do you feel you've been successful here?*

You are direct aren't you?

*I have to be, it's my job as an executive coach. How would you grade yourself on hiring your successor?*

Ouch … I guess I'd have to give myself an "F" as I haven't been able to do it so far.

*Mike, I wouldn't say that it's an "F". That would mean that you've failed. If you haven't stopped trying then I wouldn't say that you've failed. You just haven't found the right formula yet. I haven't given up on this for you yet!*

## Systems

Systems refer to all things you use to assure that what you do is repeatable, sustainable, and scalable. That means all your policies, procedures, software, and so forth fall into this category.

Let's look at what I said in the previous paragraph a little closer, as this is a critical point to achieving the *self-sustainability stage* of the growth model. I said that systems help your business become repeatable, sustainable, and scalable. What exactly does that mean?

First let's explore repeatability with a question. What makes you an expert in what you do? It's your ability to do the work and get consistent results every time. That means what you do is *repeatable*.

Having systems is the same thing. The difference is a system is documented and can be taught to others. The result is you can add others to the business and they get the same results as you when they do it.

It's not as easy as it sounds. And, this is the one area I see many business owners struggle, and where I can help because I am a systems expert. I can turn *anything* into a repeatable process. So when people listen to what I tell them, they end up with systems that others are using to get the same results.

This takes us to the second part of the system equation — sustainability. I talk about sustainability a lot. Making your business self-sustainable is what sets you free. When you have systems that can allow others to do what you do, your business has the potential to become sustainable.

Why wouldn't every business owner want to put systems in place and become sustainable as soon as possible? Good question and there are only two good answers. Either they don't know how to build systems for their business; or they are resisting doing it.

But why would they resist? Here is where psychology enters the equation. Some business owners get their self-esteem and self-worth from what they do. So if others do what they do, they feel as if they lose a part of themselves. The result is they resist.

This is one of the more difficult aspects of coaching and consulting. While most coaches and consultants are not licensed therapists, more times than you can imagine their roles are that of therapists.

Once your business is sustainable you can begin thinking about the third item — scalability. Scalability relates to Stage 4, Rapid Growth. In this stage you grow your business to a size that gives you the kind of profit that allows you to have the life that you've always dreamed of having.

The main point I am trying to make in this book is growing your business is a process. That makes business growth a system. Part of that system is making your business repeatable, sustainable, and scalable. Remember, systems must be followed in a particular order to get the outcome the system was designed to create. It's the same for using the systems in your business to achieve business growth; you must create and improve any one system in this order:

1. Repeatable
2. Sustainable
3. Scalable

## Our owners' understanding of systems

*Brandy let's start with you, what kind of systems are you focused on building as you get started?*

I'm just starting my business. It's too early to start thinking about systems — right?

*Not really. Your systems are currently in your head. You just need to stay aware so that you don't get caught up in your work and your systems never get formalized so others can use them too.*

*This is where most businesses that are stuck get stuck in the first place. They never really planned or put systems in place. The systems are all stuck in the owner's head.*

*Chris and Ann, do you have this problem?*

Now that you mention it, this is much of the problem we experience! It even causes us to argue. I get upset because the paperwork doesn't get done unless I sit down and do it. Sometimes I get angry with Chris because he doesn't help.

But now I see, how can he? He doesn't know what I do or how I do it! I need to write it down and show him what I do so if he ever needed to do it he could.

*Now you have the idea, Ann. What about you Chris, do you have problems here too?*

I sure do! If something happened to me, I don't know if anyone else could take the calls, schedule the work, and do it! We have a couple of carpet techs, but they don't know how to take calls and schedule. Ann takes calls when I can't, but she still just gives them to me to schedule. I need to get a checklist put together and teach to everyone else what to do.

*You've got it. How about Mega Power, Mike, do you have systems?*

Everything in our company has a system. That's how all our departments are able to operate independent of each other and it all seems to come together in the end. We have dozens of people all doing the same job all over the company and the results are always the same. That's pretty much your definition of a system — right?

*It is. So why can't you leave, Mike?*

Not sure, but if I put it into a context of *systems*, then I realize I haven't elevated this into our executive systems.

*Bingo! There aren't defined decision making criteria where the executive team can empower the managers and supervisors to make decisions on their own. As a result, the executives get dragged into every managerial level decision.*

*Additionally, you haven't separated you roles as executive (CEO) and owner. If you create performance objectives as an owner and communicate those to your executive team, then you could step away.*

*Lack of executive systems is a problem in many mid-sized companies. The owners wear their owner hats all the time. An owner should only play the role of owner during owner meetings. If they want to be the*

CEO, sales rep, or any other job in the company then rest of the time they should take on the responsibilities of their day-to-day role. The problem is they mix all the roles together and then have a heck of a time trying to figure out how to untangle them all when they decide to hang it up.

Wow, that's a good point! I don't have to be the CEO; someone else could take that role. I just have to tell them my expectations as the owner of the company. Then if I use the quarterly review meeting as a system of evaluating the CEO's performance I don't need to be there every day!

Sounds like you've just had an ah ha moment, Mike. Could you let go if you had a system like this in place?

Heck yeah!

Well then, see, you haven't failed like you said before. Instead, you've identified that you need to document your executive system, which will then help you find the right person to replace you and to help you to evaluate their performance.

## Business assets

Business assets are those tangible and intangible things that a business both owns and that give value to the business, such as equipment, facilities, customer lists, intellectual property, and so on.

It's usually easy to see how tangible assets, such as buildings, equipment, and even guard dogs, have value. But too frequently, business owners fail to see that they even own intangible assets, or understand that their intangible assets —things like training programs or formulas they've developed — may have even more value than their tangible ones.

In many cases, owners forget or are not aware of their intangible assets because intangibles are not listed on their balance sheets or other routine financial reports.

This makes it easy for owners like you to overlook the importance of understanding business assets, especially if you haven't yet reached the self-sustainability stage of the growth model. Until you get your processes, procedures, and quality standards documented and training developed — that is, until you create your systems — your intangibles reside in your *brain* and are not assets at all.

This is *not* good. When things are locked up in your head they have little value to others because your business is *dependent* on *you* to create its cash flow.

Among the "others" are investors and buyers of businesses; these people are interested in cash flow more than anything else. If your cash flow can be destroyed by you getting hit by a bus (yes, I brought up the "hit by a bus" scenario) you will lose the interest of more than half of your potential buyers!

But not being able to sell your business isn't the only risk; another risk is this: What happens to the most important "others" of all — your family, and those who work for you and their families — if the bus scenario becomes a reality? If your "business house" isn't in order then they are left having to cope with your death and a mess to clean up at the same time.

I hope this reinforces the importance of systems to you and your business. Too many business owners don't address the issue of creating systems as soon as they should. Not having systems introduces high risk for you, your business, and others.

Systems take time to create, test, and perfect; perhaps as long as three to five years. Why not create your systems at the beginning and have the choice to retire in three to five years if you want! Isn't that why you started your business in the first place — to be independent and financially free?

Business assets — those tangible and intangible things that you own and give value to your business — are also of real or potential value to others. But you need to manage them properly. Get started today!

## Our owners' understanding of business assets

*To give the others an idea of how this works, Mike, let start with you. How do you manage your business assets for Mega Power?*

Most of our business assets are well under control. Our systems take care of much of it. We have an extensive and well documented customer list within our ERP system; that is, our enterprise resource planning system. Our vendor relationships are all formalized with contract agreements. And, our customer service policy, which is why 93% of our customers have said they keep coming back, is formalized, and documented; and we train it religiously to all new hires.

*Wow, that is pretty impressive. Chris and Ann how do you manage your business assets?*

Our business assets are far less formalized. In fact, until we just heard you talk about this and Mike share how he does it at Mega Power, our philosophy has been "that stuff is just for big corporations."

*I guess you now see that nothing could be further from the truth. This stuff is what helps small businesses grow and become successful.*

*Let's start with something simple. How do you each of you manage your customer list? Do have a CRM system?*

What's a CRM system?

*It's a customer relationship management system. A CRM helps you manage your names and addresses; who you need to call back when; when you expect orders from existing customers and new prospects; and so forth.*

No we don't have a CRM system. But I see how that could be very helpful to us.

Our customer list is all over the place. We don't have a list of prospects. I just keep that stuff in my head and call on people when I remember to. I can really see the problem here.

We don't have a sales "hit list." As a result when we lose a customer, we scramble to replace them as soon as we can. But that means we start from scratch every time. No wonder we struggle, we're not managing our most important resource — our customers!

*Well, now that you know it you can fix it. But I do see a pattern and I hope you see it, too. Everything is a mad scramble! But it doesn't need to be. You just need a little more discipline and structure to what you do. You need some systems. And you need to begin with the basic things that are necessary for any business to operate — business assets. Your customers would be a great place to start learning how to manage a business asset.*

*What about you, Brandy? You're just getting started Does that mean you don't have any business assets yet?*

No, I don't see it that way. If I didn't have business assets then I probably would not have considered starting a business.

*That's a very enlightened perspective, Brandy! So what are your business assets at this point?*

It's my knowledge about the training systems that are out there. It's my knowledge about "how to build a better mousetrap." I think that has value!

*You're right it does. Not to everyone, but this is what real "angel investors" look to invest in. Angel investors are private investors who help startup businesses get started when the investors see that there is a great potential for return on investment (ROI).*

*Angel investors are looking for your key differentiator. You hear investors ask "What makes you different?" That's what they're looking for with that question. What is it that YOU believe gives your business VALUE? YOU are the number one business asset for your business.*

*For you Brandy, it's your knowledge like you said. Now what you need to do is show how you can make money with that knowledge. Then you have something that an investor might be interested in.*

# Chapter 7: At What Stage Are You and Your Business?

## General categories you need to assess

To this point, I've tried to demonstrate why understanding the business growth model is critical to your business's growth. We looked at the five stages and the one and only goal in each stage. By now, you should also have a good understanding of the eight factors — four in leadership and four in management — influencing your business's growth.

Hopefully, this has simplified the process of business growth for you. But now you're probably asking yourself, "Where do my business and I fall in the growth model?" or "Which factors should I be focused on?" Excellent questions and what we want to focus on next.

## Objectively assessing your growth stage

This is a good place for an example. Let me show you how to transition a business owner's knowledge from being a brain-locked *business asset to a system*. Hang with me here. You'll see the parallel quick enough.

As a management consultant, my value comes from my ability to rapidly and objectively assess a business's current situation. Then to diagnose the problems that exist and develop solutions to help correct the problems. This is what gives my business value. It is one of my *business assets*.

If I can document the assessment process so that others can do what I do, then I have transformed my business asset into a system that I can use to create self-sustainability in my business.

That's what I did with the "Small Business Growth Assessment," a tool to help you objectively assess your current stage of growth and the factors you need to focus to move to the next level of growth.

The "Small Business Growth Assessment" is a list of yes/no questions which you can quickly answer. The assessment shows you which stage of the growth model you are in, and which growth factors are your strengths or weaknesses. You can see the list of questions in appendix A.

## Our owners' and their business growth assessments

Let's see how the *Business Growth Assessment* works. The tool has been applied to our three case study businesses to objectively show the stage of each business.

You can find a complete example report in appendix B. You'll notice these reports are pretty comprehensive. You don't need all the details to see the key points which should be important to our business owners. Now let's look at how the Business Growth Assessment can help our company owners.

## Matthews Training Tech, Inc.

*So Brandy, was your score what you expected?*

Yes, I think so. I figured I would rank pretty low. The assessment shows my business is firmly in the *foundation stage* with a score of 7 out of 37.

*Based on what you've learned to this point, what do you feel like your primary goal is for your business?*

Figure out how to start making money so that I can break even as soon as possible!

*That's right. Sounds like you've got this model figured out.*

*Additionally, in which of the different influencing growth factors do you think you should focus.*

Well, the assessment has pointed out a number of weaknesses in nearly every area. So I am a little overwhelmed here. I see I need help everywhere, but what kind of help do I get and will it be too much for me to absorb with everything else I have going on?

*That's a pretty good observation. What you're experiencing is similar to what most people experience when they first start a business. It's like taking a drink from a firehose! Stay tuned. I will be showing you exactly what you need to do while you are in the foundation stage.*

# Business Growth Charts

| Growth Stages | Your Score | Max Possible |
|---|---|---|
| 1-Foundation | 3 | 5 |
| 2-Survival | 2 | 11 |
| 3-Self-Sustainability | 2 | 21 |
| **Grand Total** | **7** | **37** |

| Growth Factors | Your Score | Max Possible |
|---|---|---|
| **Owner** | **4** | **19** |
| Goals | 1 | 2 |
| Operational Skill | 1 | 5 |
| Managerial | 1 | 7 |
| Strategy | 1 | 5 |
| **Company** | **3** | **18** |
| Financial | 1 | 4 |
| Personnel | 0 | 3 |
| Systems | 1 | 7 |
| Business Asset | 1 | 4 |
| **Grand Total** | **7** | **37** |

| Business Functions | Your Score | Max Possible |
|---|---|---|
| Admin | 3 | 10 |
| Exec | 1 | 8 |
| Financial | 1 | 4 |
| HR | 0 | 6 |
| Ops | 2 | 3 |
| Sales | 0 | 6 |
| **Grand Total** | **7** | **37** |

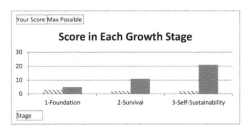

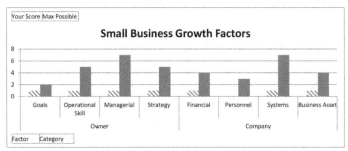

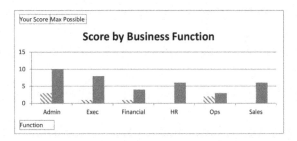

## Excellence Carpet Cleaning, Inc.

*Ann and Chris, you scored 13, almost twice that of Brandy who scored 7. Does your score seem about right to you?*

I think so. We have some of this figured out, but there is still a lot that is just up in the air.

*So based on your score, what stage of business growth do you think you are in?*

I'm not sure! We make a profit, but it's not consistent. So I kind of feel like we've got a foot in two different stages — *foundation* and *survival.*

*That's exactly right. You are in transition from the foundation stage to the survival stage.*

This make things a little dicey. What should we focus on?

*You need to make sure you have everything necessary in the foundation stage taken care of. Then begin working on things necessary to achieve the goal of the survival stage. Based on what you've learned so far to this point, what is your primary goal?*

Well, because we're sort of transitioning, we probably need to make sure that we break even every month. And, then we need to start focusing on making a consistent profit at the same time.

*That is exactly right! You did a good job in figuring this out. Real life is not as cut and dried as a model might make it seem. Life can get messy, just like business. But if you've successfully run your own business for any amount of time, you're more than smart enough to be able to figure this out. I have confidence in you!*

*Now look closely at ECC's growth factors:*

- *Management*
- *Strategy*
- *Business Assets*
- *Systems*

*Do you see what areas you need to focus on, Chris and Ann?*

It looks like *management* and *strategy* are where we really need help.

*That's right. And if you think about big businesses these things are usually associated with bigger companies. So it makes sense that if you want to grow ECC, you need to become better at these skills.*

*It also looks like you need to think about business assets and systems. Why do you think these factors would be critical for you?*

Well, these factors are associated with business self-sustainability. So if we want to achieve the self-sustainability stage we need to master these growth factors.

*You nailed it! Business assets and systems are also usually the factors that are associated with businesses that are stuck in the survival stage. Applying business assets and developing well-defined systems that use those business assets are what allow a business to operate on its own and give a business real value. We'll take a closer look at these critical areas of growth later when we talk about the survival stage.*

# Business Growth Charts

| Growth Stages | Your Score | Max Possible | Growth Factors | Your Score | Max Possible | Business Functions | Your Score | Max Possible |
|---|---|---|---|---|---|---|---|---|
| 1-Foundation | 5 | 5 | **Owner** | **4** | **19** | Admin | 4 | 10 |
| 2-Survival | 3 | 11 | Goals | 1 | 2 | Exec | 1 | 8 |
| 3-Self-Sustainability | 5 | 21 | Operational Skill | 2 | 5 | Financial | 2 | 4 |
| **Grand Total** | **13** | **37** | Managerial | 1 | 7 | HR | 2 | 6 |
| | | | Strategy | 0 | 5 | Ops | 2 | 3 |
| | | | **Company** | **9** | **18** | Sales | 2 | 6 |
| | | | Financial | 2 | 4 | **Grand Total** | **13** | **37** |
| | | | Personnel | 2 | 3 | | | |
| | | | Systems | 2 | 7 | | | |
| | | | Business Asset | 3 | 4 | | | |
| | | | **Grand Total** | **13** | **37** | | | |

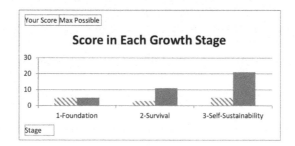

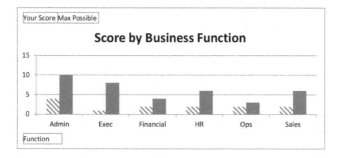

## Andrews Mega Power, Inc.

*Finally, let's look at Andrews Mega Power. Mike, your business scored 24 out of 37, which puts you squarely in the survival stage. Is this where you thought that you were?*

Well not really, I had always thought of Mega Power as a successful business. But by this criteria we're not really as successful as I thought!

*A good point and I am glad that you came to that conclusion on your own. This is usually where I get into a debate with the big "alpha dogs" about how successful they are. My opinion is you are successful, and it's your business that needs a little work. Would you agree with that, Mike?*

Absolutely!

Mike, what things stand out to you after seeing your assessment?

At first I thought "Our business is very profitable, so why isn't it scoring higher than this?" But when I go back and think about the *self-sustainability stage*, the main aspect of the *self-sustainability stage* that separates it from the survival stage is that **the business can operate on its own without the owner's involvement**. Mega Power isn't at this point yet.

*Wow Mike, that's a pretty humble observation. What do you think you and your team need to focus on to push the company to the self-sustainability stage?*

My team still looks to me for all the major decisions. While this didn't seem like a big deal, because the company is profitable, it is a big deal because the business is dependent on me and I cannot step away from it. If I tried to sell it right now I would probably get a fraction of what it's really worth.

*I'd agree with everything that you've said. The problem areas for Mega Power seem to be in the strategy, personnel, and business assets areas. If you think about it, this makes sense. The low scores in these areas seem to be due to the fact that you haven't been able to find, train, and relinquish leadership to a successor. That one key strategic factor cuts very deeply across all three of these growth factors. We will take a deeper dive into these areas of focus for you and you team when we learn how to apply the growth factors to the self-sustainability stage.*

*From this point forward, this book is laid out to show you how to apply the leadership and management growth factors based on the stage of business growth you are in.*

# Business Growth Charts

| Growth Stages | Your Score | Max Possible |
|---|---|---|
| 1-Foundation | 5 | 5 |
| 2-Survival | 9 | 11 |
| 3-Self-Sustainability | 13 | 21 |
| **Grand Total** | **27** | **37** |

| Growth Factors | Your Score | Max Possible |
|---|---|---|
| **Owner** | **11** | **19** |
| Goals | 2 | 2 |
| Operational Skill | 4 | 5 |
| Managerial | 5 | 7 |
| Strategy | 0 | 5 |
| **Company** | **16** | **18** |
| Financial | 4 | 4 |
| Personnel | 3 | 3 |
| Systems | 6 | 7 |
| Business Asset | 3 | 4 |
| **Grand Total** | **27** | **37** |

| Business Functions | Your Score | Max Possible |
|---|---|---|
| Admin | 7 | 10 |
| Exec | 3 | 8 |
| Financial | 4 | 4 |
| HR | 4 | 6 |
| Ops | 3 | 3 |
| Sales | 6 | 6 |
| **Grand Total** | **27** | **37** |

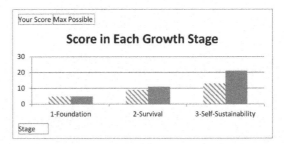

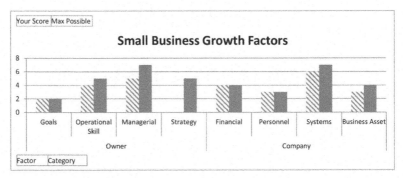

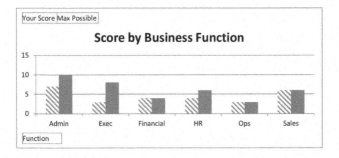

# PART II
# Simplifying Business Growth
# for
# Your Business

## Chapter 8: Assess Your Business's Stage of Growth

Now that you have seen how an objective assessment helped our case study business owners diagnose where they are in the growth model, take a closer look at your own business. Use the business growth assessment in Appendix A to see which growth stage your business is in. The diagram below will give you an idea of the questions. There is a scoring table at the end of the questionnaire to help you determine your stage of business growth.

| # | Questions | Yes/No |
|---|-----------|--------|
| 1 | Has your business reached breakeven every month for 9 months or annually 2 consecutive years? | |
| 2 | Did you originally fund your business? If no, from where did the money come? | |
| 3 | Do you currently have employees? If yes, how many people do you currently employ? | |
| 4 | Do you require equipment to produce the product/service your business delivers? | |
| 5 | When you began your business was your primary goal something other than making money? | |
| 6 | Do you have a % profit requirement which you try to achieve each month? If yes, what %? | |
| 7 | Has your business been profitable for 9 consecutive months or annually 2 consecutive years? | |
| 31 | Do you have experience selling in the market that you serve before starting this business? How many years? | |
| 32 | Do you conduct a regularly scheduled the pro/meet/service with the management team? | |
| 33 | What is the frequency of your management meetings: Daily, Weekly, Monthly, or As Needed? | |
| 34 | Does a written accounting system exist for creating proposals/quotes, ordering materials, communicating production orders, billing customers, etc.? | |
| 35 | Do you have a written or automated method of tracking all clients, prospects, and sales in process? | |
| 36 | Do you have company assets that are tracked and show up on your balance sheet? | |
| 37 | Is your product or service unique? If yes, do you have a patent or copyright filed to protect it? | |
| | **Overall Total** | |

With the canvas started for all our case study companies and your own, let's take a closer look at how each of you should handle your situation based on your stage of the growth model. We will begin by looking at the foundation stage and what Brandy, and to some extent Chris and Ann, need to do to advance their companies.

## Chapter 9: Foundation Stage Strategy

Let's dig a little deeper into what you need to do if you find yourself in the foundation stage. Remember the foundation stage does not mean that you're a startup. It means that you have not yet achieved the primary goal of the foundation stage.

*Goal: Get monthly cash flow to the point of consistent breakeven.*

No matter which stage of growth you are, you'll need to attend to the same leadership and management factors. But for any particular factor, the aspects you pay attention to will change depending on your growth stage. The tables below show what to focus on in the foundation stage.

| Leadership Factors | Focus in Foundation Stage |
|---|---|
| *Owner Goals* | • Drive growth with your vision<br>• Engage in activities that sustain passion and energy for your business |
| *Operational Skills* | • Become the expert in how to sell your product or service and how to run your operations |
| *Managerial Abilities* | • Be comfortable with trial and error |
| *Strategic Thinking* | • Write your business and action plans<br>• Review and update your plans weekly |

| Management Factors | Focus in Foundation Stage |
|---|---|
| *Financial Assets* | • Sell enough to generate breakeven cash flow every month<br>Money sources<br>• Get flexible payment terms from suppliers<br>• Sell to customers<br>• Obtain grants<br>• Get crowd funding |
| *Personnel Resources* | • Do the work yourself; do not incur debt to hire others |
| *Systems* | • Start documenting your quality standards and processes |
| *Business Assets* | • Use your own equipment and other assets; do not incur debt to buy it |

If any of these management growth factors seem foreign or unclear to you, then as a business owner, you have another growth item to address — getting some business training. If you don't know how to accomplish these growth factors, the chances of you moving forward decreases dramatically. Lack of business training is one of the reasons so many startups fail. Seek the assistance of a small business development center in your area or find a business coach (not a personal coach) to help you.

Remember, in the foundation stage your goal is to get monthly cash flow to the point of consistent breakeven. With the leadership and management growth factors as a backdrop, let's take a look at what you can begin doing to apply these factors to achieve consistent breakeven in your business.

## 4 Key objectives for creating a breakeven business

We've all heard the dire statistics: 7 out of 10 new businesses survive at least two years, and about half survive five years. What can you do to avoid being on the wrong side of these statistics?

You can (no, you *must*) focus on following a strategy that will move your business from the *foundation stage* to the *survival stage* of the small business growth model. In the foundation stage, your strategy should be to achieve four objectives:

1. Assure enough cash to meet financial needs.

2. Prove a market exists by getting enough customers so your business can survive.

3. Provide service well enough to create customer loyalty.

4. Complete the proper legal structure for your company.

To achieve any one of these four objectives, you might need to focus on improving your leadership growth factors, management growth factors, or both.

Even more important is understanding *how* focusing on these objectives will move your company to the next stage of small business growth.

### Assure enough cash to meet financial needs

This objective should be self-explanatory; but if it is, then why do so many companies go under because of lack of cash? It's because the owners don't understand the concept of cash flow. Cash flow means *money in hand* to pay bills. Not a signed contract or an invoice out the door. Depending on how long it takes you to deliver what was contracted and the terms and conditions of your order, it could take you months before you see your money!

Do you have enough cash from when you started to carry you through this timeframe? What if your plan doesn't go exactly as you think it will, then what? That's why it is important to always look at a best case and a worst case scenario. While the worst case may not happen, at least you know the range of possibilities and can plan accordingly financially.

### Prove a market exists by getting enough customers to break even

While this objective also seems quite obvious, do you really understand this objective well enough? How many customers do you need to break even every month? That is, how many customers do you need to keep the doors to your business open? If you don't know this number then you are "flying blind" and your success is left to chance.

Remember the first objective — "get enough cash." Once you know your cash target, then you must understand how many customers you need to generate the sales you need to make each month to hit your cash target. Your picture becomes clearer now and you know how much work it will take to keep the doors open.

### Provide service well enough to create customer loyalty

Now that you are getting customers you need to do whatever it takes to keep them coming back and bringing other customers to you. What does it take to make people say "Wow, I want some more, please!"

When you get your business to this point, you don't have to find new customers every month. Either they'll come back for more or send other ones to you. When you create customer loyalty, then you get some part of your second objective —prove a market exists — accomplished without working at it.

Having a loyal customer base does not mean you get to slow down your sales and marketing. Instead, it means you are now using your sales and marketing effort to attract enough customers to move you from the foundation stage (breakeven cash flow) to the survival stage (profitable cash flow).

### Create the proper legal structure

A proper legal structure is more important than for just taxes and legal purposes. It also demonstrates that you are a real business owner who is serious about what you do. Many of your prospects will investigate your business's legal status before they will place an order or even spend time talking with you. If you are serious about your business, make sure you demonstrate all the traits of a serious business. That means putting the proper legal structure in place.

Additionally, there are tax and legal obligations that come with doing business. Not having the proper legal structure creates risk and exposure to you and your family and your business. Without a proper legal structure, you could end up with surprise visits from the IRS, or from lawyers hired by your customers, competitors, or employees. Either situation could slow down your business growth or even kill your business.

## Are our owners focused on consistent, breakeven cash flow?

*Ok, so my question for you, Chris and Ann, is do you have an eye on any one of these four key objectives?*

Yes, I think we have most of these items covered pretty well. Except — like we said earlier when we were talking about managing our business assets — when we lose a customer. Then we seem to scramble to replace them. We should probably be focused on getting more customers.

*I would agree with that observation. If you keep doing it then your business will grow organically without you even trying.*

*What about you Brandy? You're the other company in the foundation stage. Are you focused on any of these objectives?*

Well, I've got my legal structure in place. But the other things are not really options right now. I need to create my software first before I can sell anything. And, if I don't have anything to sell I can't find customers.

*Well, how long will that take you? And, do you have enough time to keep your business going until you do?*

I'm not sure how long it will take me. I really need to figure it out so that I can move from foundation and get to business survival.

*Better figure it out quick or you might become one of the dire statistics. Or, might I make a suggestion, Brandy?*

Absolutely, I am all for getting this figured out sooner rather than too late.

*What if you think about your business differently at first? What if you consulted with companies trying to implement online training systems first? This would allow you to find some customers for cash flow. And, it gives you companies that might pay for you to develop your new system because they have the same problems as you have at your current employer.*

That's a good idea. I hadn't thought about doing it that way. But it makes sense if I need to achieve these objectives to get my business moving forward.

*Exactly! This is a problem I see a lot with startups. They're not focused on the right objectives and when they get around to them they've already run out of money.*

What else do I need to focus on to get paying customers? I don't want to become another statistic!

*Well, let's take a look.*

## 3 Critical sales questions you must answer in the foundation stage

Let's begin by looking at the business functions you should be focusing on during the foundation stage of growth. Because revenue is one of the most critical measures of growth let's start by looking at sales.

You already know what you need to achieve in the foundation stage:

*Goal: Get monthly cash flow to the point of consistent breakeven.*

Getting cash flow to breakeven is critical. If you can't do that your business becomes another of the millions of businesses that fail in the first five years of foundation.

In the foundation phase, sales are all about the mechanics — getting to breakeven as fast as you can. So you need to understand exactly what it takes to get there and forget about all the "bells and whistles." You can look at the sexy side of sales after your business is on solid ground!

*How many sales does it takes to break even?*

The first thing you need to know is how many sales do you need to make to break even? It's just a simple calculation, but you'd be surprised at how many small business owners, even those who are beyond this stage, understand this number.

To figure this out, calculate how much money you need to pay all the bills for your business for a month. In addition to the obvious bills such as utilities and rent, be sure to include the materials and labor to produce your service or product. Next, divide this by the *average* price for one unit of your product or service.

**Monthly Breakeven $/Average Price per Service or Product = Number of Sales per Month**

For example, a handyman needs to bring in $7,000 to pay all his bills, loans, and salary for his labor. He bills an average of $350 for a service call. Applying the formula here:

$$\$7,000 / \$350 = 20 \text{ service calls}$$

*Who buys what you sell?*

This next question gets you focused on your target market. Who buys what you sell? Is there more than one group? If so, does one group want something different than the other?

The whole point of this step is to begin refining where you will spend your time. Too often companies in the foundation stage are all over the board by trying to sell everything they could sell to everyone. This is a bad strategy. You have limited time and money. So you need to spend it where it will give you the best payoff.

Go back to our handyman example, who can he sell his services to?

- • Homeowners
- • Rental property owners
- • Property management companies

He needs 20 sales a month. If he sells to homeowners he needs a lot of homeowners as customers. If he sells to rental property owners and each owner has more than one property, then he needs fewer customers. And, if he finds a handful of property management companies, they could keep him in business all month long!

*How do you reach them?*

Now that you know who you sell to, where do these people *primarily* look to buy your type of product or service? Is it the Internet, friends, colleagues, stores, directories, or by some other means? This tells you how to engage with them so that you can get their attention. This is really more marketing than sales at this point, but you need to understand where you will find the opportunity to sell so that you can build the appropriate sales and marketing plan.

From our handyman example, property management companies, while the biggest bang for the buck, may be too big for him as he gets started. So he will target rental property owners. He may find these people by talking to realtors or by contacting people in areas where rental properties are more common than owner-occupied properties. Again, this approach is much different than trying to find individual homeowners and might require a lot of advertising.

By answering the three critical questions — how many sales to break even, who buys from you, and how do you reach them — you have all the information you need to create a solid sales plan, build a targeted list, and begin connecting so you can create interest in your product or service. Once you've answered your three critical sales questions, then finding and closing business is well within reach.

One reason you want to build your plan by answering the three critical sales questions is so you can document what you did and how you did it. You've just built a business system to help you break even every month! Once you know it works consistently, then you want to pass it on to someone else and make selling to break even their responsibility in the business. By doing this you are learning to delegate. Delegation is another critical aspect of business growth.

Let's see if our business owners have answered the three critical sales questions for their businesses.

## Checking in with our business owners

*So Brandy, how are you focused on your sales function currently?*

Well, like I said earlier, I'm not. I thought I needed to build my new online training software to have something to sell. But the consulting approach you suggested is a great way to get started! Also, it gives me real world feedback so that I can build a better system later.

*Good point, and the best thing is that it gets you creating cash flow so that you can begin achieving the goal of the foundation stage — to break even consistently — faster.*

*How about you two, Ann and Chris, do you have this level of insight into your sales and marketing?*

No, but that was pretty clear earlier, too. We don't have any insight into how many jobs we need to do every month to break even. It just sort of happens.

We know who our target customers are and I have a pretty good idea of what they want having been serving them for so long. We just need more of them!

*So how do you get more of them?*

I guess we need to get more active in our marketing and selling. We only do it when we're forced to! No wonder we just sort of hobble along! If we did what we did when we lose a customer all the time we'd have more work than we can handle. Maybe that's why we've avoided trying to get more customers; because if we did, then maybe the quality of what we offer would go down and we'd lose the customers we already have.

*This is a good insight, and it kind of leads us into our next topic — managing and expanding your operations.*

## 4 operational objectives in the foundation stage

No matter what business you are in, there are four operational areas you must address from a production perspective or business growth will eat you for lunch! And one or more are nearly always missing in businesses in the foundation and the survival stages of business growth. The four operational areas where you need to focus are to:

- Understand in detail what it takes to break even.

- Document your quality assurance processes and procedures.

- Establish a customer service policy and an infrastructure to support it.

- Gather customer and market feedback on how to improve your product or service.

These operational areas are so important in the foundation stage because they support business growth. If you don't address them at this stage, they will consume you in the later stages as you try to support both your current and your new customers.

### Get to breakeven

This first objective is focused on the goal of the foundation stage — to consistently break even. Many small business owners don't even know this number; much less have a plan to get there!

My assignment for all clients at the foundation stage is to build a detailed plan of what needs to happen to consistently break even every month for a simple, powerful reason: so you can delegate the breakeven responsibility to someone else. This frees you up to focus on more critical aspects of the business to move it from the foundation stage and in to the survival stage of growth.

## Consistently assure quality

If you ask business owners about outsourcing to build capacity, many grimace in agony. More small business owners fail than should because the owners don't show their vendors how a delivered product or service should look. They leave too much to chance and then are surprised by the result they get.

If you have a product that you manufacture, quality assurance comes in the form of a specification. It's a plan the product is built to and that the delivered product's quality is measured against.

For a service, this is an operating procedure on how a service technician or representative is expected to deliver what you sell. When you document your operating procedure you can evaluate what is delivered, as can the customer. Make sure it matches with what your marketing materials and contract say, and you cover yourself from unexpected complaints.

## Provide real customer service

Why do you need to provide real customer service when you are still only in the foundation stage? Because if you are not thinking about it from the beginning, you will create problems before you even start. Remember, to consistently achieve breakeven cash flow, you need loyal customers who give you repeated sales and who refer you to others.

A customer service policy is actually a critical part of defining the "persona of your business" to your prospects, customers, and employees. It tells prospects and customers exactly how you will treat them. If you say you provide superior service in your literature, you'd better deliver on that promise or you will have an even a bigger problem: a bad reputation in the market.

Your customer service policy also tells the employees you have and the ones you want to hire what is expected of them and sets the tone for their performance evaluations. There is nothing worse than getting bad hires from the start. It take months or even years to recover from a bad decision in hiring.

*Get market feedback*

You started your business with assumptions about what you could profitably sell and who would buy it.

When you close every sale, remember to ask your customer why they bought the product or service, and why they bought it from you. Don't hope they'll volunteer the information. The answers they give you will be great feedback on how you can provide more of what the market wants.

The best marketing skill in the foundation stage is listening to what customers tell you. This is a good way to get that feedback without spending more money to get it. Your installers or service reps are engaging with the customer. Make sure they are listening to what the customers are saying and reporting it back to you.

Don't be afraid to ask your customers what they think. If you don't ask, you'll miss out on an opportunity to grow faster. Good feedback in the foundation stage will help you identify and solve the problems that are stunting your business growth. Solving problems in the foundation stage will help you move more quickly into and through the survival stage. Taking care of foundational objectives in the foundation stage is often the difference between getting to the self-sustainability stage in three years instead of five. So how fast do you want success?

## Checking in with our owners

*So, Ann and Chris, how do you handle your operations? Have you implemented any of these operational objectives into your service delivery?*

Well, yes and no. We get compliments on our service all the time. In fact, we've had past clients come back to us after going to another carpet cleaner for a lower price. They usually say it's not worth the number of callbacks that they end up making with the lower priced cleaner. So we deliver good service.

*Some, but not all, customers tell us about their service experiences when they call us. So we're not actively soliciting this information. And, it's not part of our customer service policy to ask.*

We train our techs on how to clean and they usually do a pretty good job. But again we're not evaluating them against a standard. So, yes, we can get better at this.

*Brandy what about you, have you thought about your operational objectives?*

Yes, I hire developers for projects all the time. I usually develop a requirements document and sometimes a design document before I begin the hiring process. Then I make my payments to the development company based on their progress against the timeline we agree to.

*Wow, sounds like you've got a great start on this. You just need to make sure that you apply that same process for your business for both external resources and for internal employees.*

That's what I'm not sure about. I know how to do it for a software developer, but how do I do it for a sales rep or an accountant?

*Great question! Stay tuned and we'll talk about that a little later when we discuss creating accountability, a crucial factor in becoming self-sustainable.*

## Putting it all together

Now, a lot of people will say, "Dino, this is way too soon for this stuff." But I disagree. It is in your foundation stage that your business growth habits are formed or not.

If you create bad business habits now, later you will not have time to think about how to replace those habits with better ones. So you will just react. As a result you will have to stop progress to deal with issues. Also, your employees will develop bad habits that will be difficult or even impossible to break.

Growing a business is a straightforward process, but it's not the path typically taken. That's why so many businesses fail. If you are just getting started or struggling in the foundation stage, I recommend that you read this book with a serious mind to use it as a guide. You will discover some of the less discussed topics are the difference between success and failure in a business. Don't leave your business to chance. Learn and apply what you need to have the success you seek.

# Chapter 10: Survival Stage Strategy — Getting Unstuck from Nowhere Land

Owners who have been in business more than three years often find themselves stuck in survival. Some recognize it, and far too many do not because they lose sight of or don't know the goal of survival.

*Goal: Consistently achieve owner-established profit requirement.*

But beware: you can be profitable in the money sense and still be stuck in the survival stage.

To do a quick check on whether you are stuck in the survival stage, here is your litmus test.

*Litmus test: Can you step away from your business right now and will it continue to generate a level of profitability that does not impact your lifestyle or that of your employees?*

If your answer is an absolute "Yes!" then congratulate yourself and finish reading this chapter while reflecting on the smart things you did to get out of survival and on your way to self-sustainability.

If you answer is "Definitely not" or "Sort of; it would take me a little time to get my house in order" then your business is not self-sustainable. You are stuck in survival or what I also call "nowhere land" because — although you are profitable — your profits depend on your everyday involvement.

If you want to be able to choose what personal independence and financial freedom mean to you, then you cannot let your profits depend on you. You need to formalize and delegate responsibility for your systems.

Don't be the owner who figures it out too late that you are still in survival when you're ready to retire. Because figuring it out too late means you'll have to work another three to five years to get out of survival.

## Why owners get stuck in survival

The reason so many owners get stuck in survival is they are lulled into a false sense of security. Their sense of security comes from having some level of financial success. However, their financial success is still dependent on their ability to get up and go to their business every day.

It is this dependence on the owner that is the ever so subtle difference between a business in survival and one in self-sustainability, because it's the self-sustainable business that makes it possible for you to have choices.

For example, suppose you envision selling your business. Will you be ready to sell when the market is ready to buy? And if yes, how much will a buyer pay? Understand this: Your business's true value to a buyer is based on your profit and your systems for generating that profit.

The same is true if you want to grow your business, and you need investors. Investors don't have any interest in running your business. They want the cash flow stream. If that cash flow stream is dependent on you then investors will have far less, if any, interest in your business.

Or maybe you have no intention of selling or scaling your business. Instead, maybe you envision keeping your business at a certain profitability level so you can enjoy a certain life style now and then passing your business to your children. Or even donating to some greater good. This is the idea of social entrepreneurship.

## Growth factors that get you out of survival

If you have money and all the stuff money can buy, you're successful, right? That depends on your definition of success.

Why did you start your own business? If you're like most business owners, you want independence and financial freedom. In the survival stage you may or may not have financial freedom; however, you certainly don't have independence in your life. In fact, you are a prisoner of your business!

So let's remember what survival really means:

*Consistently achieve owner-established profit requirement.*

And here are the tables to show you what to focus on in the survival stage.

| Leadership Factors | Focus in Survival Stage |
|---|---|
| *Owner Goals* | • Set a profit requirement and use it for planning<br>• Continue driving growth with your vision<br>• Continue engaging in activities that sustain passion and energy |
| *Operational Skills* | • Continue being the expert in how to sell your product or service and how to run your operations<br>• When you are consistently profitable, then hire one key manager |
| *Managerial Abilities* | • Start training and delegating work while keeping primary control<br>• Continue being comfortable with trial and error |
| *Strategic Thinking* | • Plan business growth based on forecasts of monthly cash flows<br>• Continue weekly reviews and updates of business and action plans |

| Management Factors | Focus in Survival Stage |
|---|---|
| *Financial Assets* | • Sell enough to make a profit every month<br>• Accurately forecast monthly cash flow<br><br>Money sources: Continue to ...<br>• Get flexible payment terms from suppliers<br>• Sell to customers<br>• Obtain grants<br>• Get crowd funding Banks will consider you under the right conditions |
| *Personnel Resources* | • Hire sales people and operational resources as necessary.<br>• Begin identifying the sales people who are loyal, high producers |
| *Systems* | • Continue documenting your quality standards and processes<br>• Begin training personnel on how to use your systems |
| *Business Assets* | • Begin to solidify a market<br>• Increase business assets, as needed, so production keeps pace with increasing sales |

## Getting out of survival means delegating

Notice most of the objectives for getting out of survival center on getting yourself untangled from the day-to-day tasks of your business. Often systems — the processes, procedures, and standards for running a business — do exist at this stage; however, the systems are just not formalized. This may be because the owner doesn't feel comfortable letting go and delegating. Is this the case in your business?

If you want any hope of moving out of survival, then you have to get comfortable with letting go. You have to take four steps to formalize your systems so that you can confidently delegate to others. The four steps for formalizing each of your business systems are:

1. Document the system.

2. Teach someone else to do it.

3. Delegate it to them.

4. Monitor it through some form of regular reporting.

Easy enough, right?

Sure, until you add the emotional attachment many owners have to their business. Often the business is a source of their self-identity. Now making the necessary changes is not so easy!

It can take decades to master the skill necessary to assist a business owners through this transition. Sometimes it can take years to get them to the point of letting go. Other owners never make it. Usually this is because they can never get past the business as being their self-identity. They never seem to define a strong enough personal goal to motivate them to make the personal changes necessary to give them another self-identity.

It truly saddens me to see this. It usually comes down to a person not having a strong enough personal relationship with anyone. They can't see themselves having fun with another person or a group of people. So their business becomes their psychological escape. It's difficult for a business coach or consultant to help these individuals. They need a *real* psychological professional.

This is why the first step in our SPARC process is to define your personal goal. Without a personal goal you don't have enough motivation to make the changes necessary in yourself to get your business unstuck.

So if you have the motivation to change personally, and you have the roadmap of the leadership and management growth factors to get there, what else do you need to get started?  Let's answer that by checking in our business owners.

## Can our business owners get beyond survival?

*Mike, how would you classify yourself?*

Well, the goal for survival is to be consistently profitable, and we definitely are. And I think we have all of the management factors under control.  But no question, Mega Power is definitely *stuck* in survival.

*So why do you think that you're stuck?*

I hate to say it, but as the business owner I'm not using my power and authority to do whatever it takes to get us out of survival and into self-sustainability.

*Wow, that's a pretty serious admission Mike!  Why do you think that you haven't taken the necessary actions to move Mega Power out of survival so it can be self-sustainable?*

For at least two reasons.  One, although my CPA, financial planner, lawyer, banker, and other advisors all said that I should think about an exit strategy, they never pointed out that survival is not the same as self-sustainability.  And two, I haven't really been ready to let go, which means I'm the biggest reason my business is still in survival.

*Did you use that terminology for a reason?*

What terminology do you mean?

*You said "I wasn't ready to let go."*

I just meant I wasn't ready to retire. So I thought I had to stay seriously, hands-on involved with everything.

*Well, the fact that you said, "let go" is important.  It may mean that there is something subconsciously going on here that you're not even aware of.  Have you tried to make a succession transition before now?*

I have had consultants in to fix the business in the past.  They didn't seem to think anyone was willing to step up and take charge so every major decision is still brought to me.  Do you think they were just telling me what I wanted to hear?

*It's possible. I would hope that any good consultant could help you with an executive hire or develop one of your existing managers into your replacement. But maybe I ask too much of a consultant.*

I don't think it's too much. If you call yourself a management consultant then you should be able to do anything that is management related.

*I agree with you, Mike. We might have to look more closely at how decisions are currently made at Mega Power. Also, it may be important to talk to others in key roles in Mega Power about how you handled recent decisions. We want to see what others think might be going on. It may be something simple that can be fixed or maybe that deeper emotional attachment is what's keeping you chained to the business.*

I'm sure Cathy would like to know what the problem is and how I am going to fix it.

*You're probably right, Mike.*

## 5 Steps to formalizing your business systems

In order to move from survival into self-sustainability, you need to master a five-step process for formalizing your systems. The process is pretty simple:

1. Do it
2. Document it
3. Test it
4. Train it
5. Delegate it

Sounds simple enough, so why do so many business owners struggle with doing it? There are a number of reasons. But I think it's more they don't understand how to do these five steps. If you ever want to be free of your business, this is a process you must master and do for every aspect of your business.

### Do it

This is the easiest step because most business owners are action oriented driver-types. Once you've completed something enough times you've pretty much settled on a process that works. You've worked out the all the kinks. You know the objections. You know the gotchas. This is usually where most people stop.

You see this all the time. One of the problems you frequently hear from owners is "nobody can do it except me!" That's because they stopped at step 1 in the process.

### Document it

This means writing down what you do. A checklist is a good place to start. My first job out of college was as a missile launch officer. We had a checklist for everything. If they use this for something as critical as launching nuclear missiles, why don't you think it will work for your business?

A workflow diagram is a good idea too. Many people learn better by seeing a visual picture. I fall into this category. I can read a page over and over and not get it. Show me a flow chart and I can do it like I am a pro who has been doing it for years!

### Test it

This step frequently gets skipped. Just because it's written down doesn't mean it works. Testing your system makes sure someone can read the instructions and get the desired outcome by doing the steps.

As many years as I have been doing this, I still get caught! I'll write a procedure and nobody can understand what I meant in one or more of the steps. When you ask, people are usually willing to tell you what confused them. Correct it and move on.

### Train it

Training seems trivial in many cases, but you'll get better results if you do. It's not just about teaching someone how to do something. It's about connecting with the person. Showing them that what they do is important enough to take the time to work with them.

You also learn a lot about a person while working with them. You get to know their learning style. How they process information. You may also discover other talents they have that you weren't aware of. This could prove advantageous later on, but if you don't take the time you'll never know.

Finally, training gives you an opportunity to see what additional things may need to be added to your procedure or what other assistance the employee may need. Remember Chris and Ann, the owners of

Excellence Carpet Cleaning a.k.a. ECC? When we checked in on them in the previous chapter — about foundation strategy — they realized that asking for customer feedback about quality is a great way to find out where they need to do a better job of training their employees.

Here's another example of why you should take the time to work with —or "train with" — your employees: you will likely uncover cultural-specific things you can do to elevate customer satisfaction.

Training will give you a *lot* of good feedback!

### *Delegate it*

This is ultimately where every owner needs to get — delegation! It is a skill lacking in many small business owners. If you've never been a manager in a bigger company, then you may never have had to delegate. But if your goal is to have a self-sustainable business, then you *will* need to delegate everything you do in your business.

This is one of those areas where business owners frequently get stuck. Often it's not the mechanics of delegation that gets them stuck. It's their mental state — the inability to let go.

Remember how I mentioned previously that many owners get too much of their self-worth from the business? It's not hard to understand why. Their business is like a child they've birthed and grown themselves. It's hard for parents to let their child wander off on their own.

If you have this tight "can't let go" grip on your business, then you have to face your demon. Start delegating now! If you don't you'll always be chained to your business, and business self-sustainability will remain a dream.

## Creating repeatability and sustainability with our owners

*So do any of you have written, tested and trained processes in your business?*

This is a place where Chris and I are stuck. We train carpet techs when they start, but it's not a very smooth process. We're always a little on pins and needles for a while when training is done. How do we know that the techs are really following the process after training is over? We tend to get more callbacks from customers for new techs than we do from Chris's jobs.

*Ok, what if you created a checklist with all the potential services completed for a carpet cleaning? After the tech has completed the job, they show the checklist of completed services to the customer. Then the customer inspects the work while the tech if still there. Now you get instant feedback and the tech can correct any problems before they leave! Additionally, if you and Chris know that the customer is holding the tech accountable for their work, then you get a better sense of comfort that the new techs are following the process.*

*If your quality standards are not part of your cleaning checklist, then you are assuming that everyone has the same knowledge as you. If you don't use a checklist, how will you ever know how well a job was done? You've probably seen it a hundred times before. Sometimes just a simple change can make a huge difference!*

Wow, that's a pretty good idea. And, it's not really that complicated, so it would be easy enough to make part of a cleaning! We even get feedback from the customer, right then and there. Having a checklist will help us take care of issues right away instead of when we bill the customer.

## 5 critical sales objectives in the survival stage

Let's begin looking functionally at what you should do within the survival stage. Because revenue is one of the most critical measures of business growth, let's start by looking at sales.

### Document your sales process

In the previous section, I stressed the importance of documenting your systems so that you can delegate. Your sales process is a system that you need to document.

You should do this to account for everything that works and everything that does not work for sales. This will be important as you begin growing. You will add more sales reps at some point, which means, you need to train them on what to do and more importantly what *not* to do.

There never seems to be time to document your sales process when you need to hire sales reps. The owner has so many things going on that they can't get the sales process committed to paper so it can be shared with others. As a result, every sales rep ends up going through the same learning over and over. This is not a scalable sales model and slows your growth and business self-sustainability.

If you document what you do and don't do —and why — then someone can go through your notes. They can organize the good stuff and list the things to avoid. Both will accelerate learning with the sales team and your sales growth when the time comes.

### Validate your market research

You didn't just run out and start selling. You researched your market. You looked at what the market wanted and what the competition was doing. From there you came up with your product or service.

Sales are where the rubber meets the road. As you begin selling, you'll get real-world feedback to your research and the decisions you made. This is another reason to document. See what assumptions you made were right, and which ones need to be adjusted. The end result is a better marketing plan and product or service that will manifest itself in more sales!

### Determine your conversion rate

You have probably heard the adage "sales is a numbers game." This is very true, so you want to pay close attention to the following sales key performance indicators, or KPIs:

- How many leads does it take to get a prospect who wants a proposal?
- How many proposals does it take to close a sale?

This is similar to getting to breakeven in the foundation stage. To get to breakeven, you focus on cash forecasting. The difference here, in survival, is that you want to start generating profit. Now, in addition to cash forecasting, you are focusing on the number of sales you need to hit your profit margin target.

Figure this out creates what's call your sales funnel. The management model mentioned previously, "Tuning Your Revenue Engine," can provide you with the formulas necessary to make these calculations. You can find additional business growth resource in Appendix E.

*Learn about and develop ways to overcome objections*

To become an entrepreneur you need to develop a thick skin! People will tell you "No!" all the time. To become comfortable handling "No," listen to the objections people give you during sales calls.

Over time you'll begin to hear the same objections over and over again. Also, you will develop ways to overcome these objections. Many times the process itself — listening and explaining — will help you make the sale.

Document the objections and how you respond when you hear them. Again, this helps you transfer your knowledge to the sales reps you hire who will help you begin to grow.

*Use customer input to improve your pitch*

When you first started selling, you made assumptions on why you think customers will buy. After you begin making sales, you have a better source than your assumptions — your customers! So ask them.

Most businesses are amazed by what they hear when they ask the question "Why do you buy our product or service?" Get enough customers to answer and patterns emerge. If you use this information in your marketing message you'll begin to find more customers like the best ones. These are the ones that you really want.

So use and document this process — asking customers why they buy from you — to make more sales with better customers.

## Creating sustainable sales

The point to the above five sales actions is to *use your intangible resources* to improve your business. As you move your business up the growth model, you will learn more about every aspect of yourself and your business. The better you become at sharing your knowledge, the more your knowledge becomes part of your business's corporate knowledge and ultimately culture.

Most businesses that don't find ways to share corporate knowledge find themselves reinventing the wheel over and over again. This stifles growth. You, as the owner, get dragged into things you don't need to be involved in because nobody else has the knowledge necessary to make decisions or get the work done. Before you know it, you've reached your limit and your business stagnates because of you.

## An example for sales expansion

*Chris and Ann what are you struggling with when it comes to sales?*

We want to begin expanding into residential work. So we need to delegate the new and existing commercial sales to our commercial manager.

*OK, so how do you think you want to begin making that transition?*

Well, I can make a commercial sale in my sleep. But how do I train someone else to do it? I have no sales management experience.

*You need to follow the five-step process for establishing a repeatable and sustainable business from earlier. "Do" is the first step. So what is the second step?*

Document it. But I don't want to have to sit down for days or weeks on end trying to document everything I do in a sale call.

*How about if you have the new guy, do the documenting?*

This is a very good idea! *Delegate* the documenting of the sales process to the sales person; I like that I idea a lot!

The person we brought in has experience in sales management. He worked at a bank and another marketing company in sales. So this will help me out tremendously. Heck, he probably knows more about it than I do anyway.

*You could be right. He might have some general sales techniques that could help ECC.*

## 3 marketing steps to consistent profits in the survival stage

The goal of the survival stage is to become consistently profitable; so it makes sense that marketing's primary objective will be to generate leads that turn into sales. Often this is a struggle for small business owners. But it doesn't have to be.

Here are the three things you need to do to strategically align your marketing with achieving consistent profitability:

1. Calculate and monitor your marketing efficiency and effectiveness.

2. Scale your current marketing plan based on your marketing key performance indicators (KPIs).

3. Add marketing campaigns to your marketing mix to meet any shortfalls

*Calculate your marketing efficiency and effectiveness*

Monitoring is a critical part of every aspect of your business. This is no different for marketing. You need to measure how well your current marketing efforts are performing so that you can evaluate if your new marketing campaigns are more effective than your current campaigns in generating leads.

There are two critical marketing metrics to use as KPIs. Each provides you with insight as to how well your marketing is performing for you.

The first marketing metric is marketing efficiency, which tells you how well your marketing resources are working for you in generating leads. You want this number to be low. The lower it is the less it is costing you to generate leads for your product or service.

You calculate marketing efficiency by dividing the *number of leads* during a period of time by the *amount of time spent* on marketing during the period. For example, if a company received 30 calls during a week and spent five hours marketing during the same week then their lead efficiency would be as follows:

**Marketing Efficiency = hours spent marketing calls / # of leads**

**.17 hours marketing per call = 5 hours marketing / 30 leads**

The second marketing metric is marketing effectiveness, which tells you how well your message is targeted. That is, are you saying the right things to the right people to generate your leads? If you find your marketing effectiveness is too low, then you need to hone your message, your target market, or both.

You calculate marketing effectiveness by dividing the number quotes or proposals you gave by the number of leads you received. Continuing with the marketing efficiency example, suppose that for every 30 leads your sales reps get, they send out 22 quotes. So you would calculate their marketing effectiveness as follows:

**Marketing Effectiveness  =  # of quotes or proposals / # of leads**

**.73 quotes per call = 22 quotes / 30 calls**

Monitoring and managing your marketing efficiency and effectiveness KPIs will help you improve profitability. Those KPIs will also provide you with the information you need for scaling your marketing plan.

*Scale your current marketing plan, but only when you need to*

This is yet another step that small business owners skip. As a result, they lose out on a lot of extra leads and spend way more than is necessary on new marketing tactics.

Based on your pervious revenue target and calculations, you should be able to determine how many more sales you need. Now you want to determine how much you need to "turn up your marketing faucet" to get the number of leads you need to generate sales.

Look at the reality of these numbers compared to your marketing budget to determine if this is realistic or not. Can you just spend more time and money doing what're already doing to generate enough leads to reach your sales goal? If you can get there just doing that, then that's your marketing plan and your plan is done!

Maximize your return on investment (ROI) on what you know first before you begin testing new ideas. Being profitable means you want to minimize expenses. So do what you can using what you already know works. When it's not working anymore, then move on, adding and testing new stuff in your marketing mix!

*Add marketing campaigns when leads fall short*

If your marketing effectiveness calculation leaves you short on leads to achieve your sales goal, then you need to add new campaigns to your marketing mix.

As you add campaigns, make sure that each is a part of an integrated marketing plan. To help ensure you have a scalable marketing plan — and to avoid needless complications — add, test, and monitor only one campaign at a time. This lets you establish a sound foundation from which you can measure the next campaign.

More often than not, your marketing efficiency and effectiveness will be worse if you try to add more than one campaign at a time. So don't. Add new marketing campaigns slowly so you cautiously monitor what you're doing and adjust quickly to things that are improving your marketing efficiency and effectiveness.

## Real world example of marketing in the survival stage

*So Chris and Ann, what are you doing with marketing in survival that gets you closer to self-sustainability in ECC?*

One reason we haven't grown is that we don't really understand marketing. We've been guilty of trying every new marketing idea that comes along and nothing seems to help.

*I hear you. This isn't an unusual scenario. In fact, it is probably the norm. Part of the problem is you didn't know how to measure your marketing success.*

That's on target. Once we learned about measuring marketing efficiency and effectiveness we did a look-back. One problem we saw immediately is we didn't know how many leads were coming in! We weren't keeping track of how many calls we get each week. Also, we weren't keeping track of how or where the people who called found out about ECC.

*If you don't know how much volume you have from each marketing tactic that you are using, then how do you know what's working and what's not? You don't. That is a big problem. So what did you and Chris do to fix the problem?*

We used paper and kept tick marks on the sheet as the daily calls came in. Each week we added the tick marks and compared it to the previous weeks. It wasn't sophisticated but it gave us an incredible picture of what was actually going on.

*So what did you learn from keeping track of your calls?*

After getting a few weeks of data we saw that we are generating about $10,000 in revenue based on the marketing we're doing right now, which is nearly nothing.

*OK great, you know that if you don't do anything then you can expect $10,000 per month. But you're goal is higher than that. It was $15,000 per month if I recall, so how did you increase your marketing from there?*

Next, we tried to add some simple things like mailing post cards. Chris also started making a conscious attempt to stop by all the properties that we have in our accounting system at least once a month.

*That's a pretty simple start, what effect did that have on your revenue?*

Before we knew it, we picked up two new properties and the number of calls has nearly doubled on a weekly basis. So we know our additional marketing efforts have paid off.

Our revenue has increased too! The next two months we saw a revenue increase to $11,500 and then $13,300 the next month.

*It sounds like things are beginning to heat up for ECC.*

## How to profitably refine your operation in the survival stage

Consistent profitability is the goal of the survival stage. So your focus, operationally, needs to be on increasing efficiency and productivity. If you can do what you do faster, you can improve cash flow which in turn helps profitability.

But to do things faster you have to already know exactly what you are doing so you can refine and fine tune it. And that's why in the foundation stage it's so important to work on consistently assuring quality. If you don't already have a standard method that assures quality and customer services systems to deal with exceptions, then it becomes nearly impossible to fine tune your operation.

When businesses get stuck in survival, it's often because they can't keep up with growing sales because they spend so much time trying to solve quality issues, find production resources, or both. So they can't keep up with sales and they stop moving forward.

If you haven't established protocols for your operation, then your business growth stops until your operation catches up. By having operating procedures that you can count on people to follow, you can:

- Know what to expect of people based on past performance.
- More rapidly train new employees to add needed capacity.
- Begin refining your system to do things faster and more cost effectively.

The "Tuning Your Revenue Engine" model, mentioned earlier, helps you identify chokepoints so you can increase throughput. Increasing throughput in-turn increases cash flow which always has good results.

So if you didn't handle the operational objectives you should have in the foundation stage, then you'll have to do it now because you aren't in survival at all; you are, in fact, still in foundation. Some people believe that the operational objectives in foundation are too early in the small business growth simplified model. But if you wait, you *will* stall in the survival stage. As a result, you may never find your way out and be stuck in survival for 10, 15, 20 years or more, just like too many other businesses.

## Examples of operational challenges

*Mike, you are growing and expanding at Mega Power. Do you have any operational challenges?*

Oh yeah. In fact Bill Constantine, my VP of production, has more than one set of challenges on his plate right now. Mega Power had to expand operations as we are critically close to capacity in production and sales doesn't seem to be slowing in the slightest.

*Ok, so how are you approaching solving you capacity problem?*

I saw some new technologies and equipment at a recent industry trade show and passed the information onto Bill. So Bill is completing a cost-benefit analysis of this new technology.

*So where are you in the process now?*

Bill completed an initial set of requirements that he and his floor manager and line supervisors helped to review and consolidate. Bill met with me to review the requirements and I gave my approval.

Next Bill completed an extensive cost-benefit analysis of the current technologies we are using and the new technology I had brought to his attention.

*What did Bill and his team find out?*

While the new technology had some real benefits, there were a number of unknowns that created some concerns for Bill and his team.

*Like what?*

Well, the additional ongoing maintenance costs of the new technology was estimated to be 7% - 12% more than our existing setup. According to Bill, the biggest problem is the fact that the product, once out the door, could not be supported by our current support team. We'd need to add another help desk for this, as well as train our third party installers on how to deal with the new technology. This doubled the cost of the expansion.

*So how does a current setup compare to the new technology?*

Bill and his team recommended that we should stick with our existing setup for this expansion; in other words, don't buy any new technology. Expanding will be far less work and cost a fraction of the new technology. On the other hand, Bill also said that sales were piling up and without this new setup production orders will go from three to seven days to more than two weeks to produce.

*So I guess you decided to scrap the idea of going with the new technology for now and just add another current setup - right?*

Well, think about how great it would be for Mega Power to be on the cutting edge with this new technology. The additional cost now is really an investment in the future of Mega Power! I am more than willing to sign off on more than what Bill and his team are requesting to be the market leader. So I asked Bill to go back and take a closer look at the new technology and let me know how they could make the new technology work.

*Wow, really? Bill and his team seem to be getting farther and farther behind with production. Sales are piling up. And, sales is saying that they don't see it letting up and you want to go in a new direction right now?*

Well, sure it's the perfect time to do it. We have plenty of money and it's what will secure us as a market leader into the next decade.

*While I understand that Mike, you need to look at what your current challenges are and make decision that help you solve those.*

What do you mean? This solves our production issue once it's up and running.

*I don't disagree with that. But there are two current challenges that you are working on. First, trying to solve your capacity challenge; and second, and more importantly, figuring out how to extract yourself from the day-to-day decision making of the company. Wouldn't you agree?*

Yes!

*Well, you asked Bill to present a solution. Which he did. Then you changed the evaluation criteria, by adding "being a market leader" to the mix, after the fact. And, you cut his knees out from under him by changing the evaluation criteria. On top of that, you sent him back to his team to work on a completely new set of requirements which only kicks their current problems farther down the road.*

*I think you may have found out the problem as to why your executive team isn't stepping up on making major decisions.*

Wow — this is a kick in the gut! But when you put it that way, you are probably right.

*Well, Mike, let's see how you can begin to correct this new found challenge of your own making.*

# Chapter 11: Self-Sustainability Stage Strategy

The self-sustainability stage of the growth model is a unique place to be. In fact, it's so unique there are two goals from which to choose. When you arrive here you get a choice for all your hard work in creating a successful business and life.

When you reach the self-sustainability stage your choices are:

*Goal Path A. Sustain the business's success created to this point.*

*or*

*Goal Path B. Rapidly grow the business to a large corporation.*

When you reach this stage of business growth you are finally independent and financially free. That is, if you really *are* in the self-sustainability stage and *not* stuck in the nowhere land of survival.

Sorry to be negative at this point. However, too many business owners are lulled into thinking they have a successful business because it's profitable. If that profitability cannot be sustained *without* you, then you are *not* in the self-sustainability stage.

Don't get me wrong; business owners with a profitable company are successful. But they only have personal success, *not* business success. Business success comes from system-generated cash flow that doesn't require owner involvement for it to occur.

Too frequently business owners have a false sense of security. Their egos get the best of them. Most won't listen to anyone until a life-altering event occurs that nearly destroys them, their family, or their business. You can identify these owners in ten minutes or less of meeting them, once you understand the difference between the survival and self-sustainability stages.

Usually they've made a decision to have what many trusted advisors call a lifestyle business. This means they chose goal path A, to sustain the business's success created to this point. The problem is they fail to realize their business hasn't yet reached the self-sustainability stage. So they forget to continue working on the eight growth factors that will get them out of survival and into self-sustainability.

Think of someone you know who has had a business for more than ten years and who you believe is still chained to their business. With what you have learned to this point from this book about how a business matures as it grows, can you diagnose their problem or problems?

The reason they are stuck is because they don't have the knowledge you have. If you, like me, thrive on helping others, you need to bring why they're stuck to their attention. You might even want to share this book with them when you are done.

With all this said, in self-sustainability — as with earlier stages and shown in the next tables — you'll continue to focus on certain aspects of leadership and management factors and you have new things to focus on.

| Leadership Factors | Focus in Self-Sustainability Stage |
| --- | --- |
| *Owner Goals* | Choose your next goal:<br>• sustain success to this point *or*<br>• move to rapid growth |
| *Operational Skills* | • Transition from "doer" to executive<br>• Delegate responsibilities to supervisory staff |
| *Managerial Abilities* | • Stop using trial and error<br>• Continue to train and delegate |
| *Strategic Thinking* | Envision 3-5 years from now. If your goal is to:<br>• sustain success, then plan your exit strategy<br>• rapid growth, then plan your growth strategy |

| Management Factors | Focus in Self-Sustainability Stage |
|---|---|
| *Financial Assets* | If your goal is:<br>• sustain success, then preserve capital, and create passive income<br>• rapid growth, then use retained earnings and cash flow to leverage growth<br>Money sources: Continue with earlier sources and add ...<br>• Banks<br>• Partnerships<br>• Leasing options |
| *Personnel Resources* | • Hire supervisory staff<br>• Hire or continue hiring employees to meet sales demand |
| *Systems* | • Use more sophisticated accounting and management systems<br>If your goal is:<br>• sustain success, then formalize your systems<br>rapid growth, then create scalable systems |
| *Business Assets* | If your goal is:<br>• sustain success, then use business assets to create passive income<br>• rapid growth, then acquire assets needed to grow |

## How big is big enough for self-sustainability?

Do you hope to take a vacation some day and not worry if your business will still be there when you return? This is something most small business owners worry about as much as they do being able to cover payroll and pay their bills every month The problem is, not many owners are working at getting their business to self-sustainability or even know how to do it.

As you've read to this point, business self-sustainability is what most business owners really want. What is it about achieving business self-sustainability that moves you into the self-sustainability stage?

It's simply this: put the people and systems in place so that the business can operate without you being there. You don't have to grow the business as big as you think to make it self-sustainable. Let's take a look.

# What's big enough for our owners?

*So, Ann and Chris, how big do you think you need to grow ECC to allow it to run on its own?*

We've really never thought about it. But I guess several million dollars.

*Well that may be true but we can figure it out quickly here just by answering a few questions. On average, what percent of net profit is ECC capable of generating on an annual basis?*

We have made as much 30% and as little as 0%. But if we had to say on average we'd hope to get a 25% net profit consistently from the business.

*Ok, and how much do you two want as an annual income so you don't need to worry about having what you want and being able to do what you want with your life?*

We began by deciding how much money we want annually to live the lifestyle of our dreams. We know that we're still young and still raising our family. We are a Christian family and live our lives pretty modestly, so we figure $60,000 a year would give us what we want at this point. We would just like to enjoy the kids while they're still young.

*I think this is a pretty admirable goal. Not enough people think this way until it's too late. For your target net profit margin and income goal, the calculation is easy:*

### Desired Annual Net Profit $ / Target Net Profit Margin = Required Total Revenue

*So applying the formula to your case we get:*

### $60,000 / 25% = $240,000

That's it? $240,000 in total annual revenue? That's not the millions that we originally thought it would take! In fact, this actually seems more than possible to us!

*You will need to look at a few other things. How much work can your current operation — personnel, equipment, and so on — really handle? If it's less than what you currently have, you have to calculate how much you need to increase your expenses and add that amount to your projected revenue.*

Well, we figure we need two more techs and another truck; that would add about another $60,000 - $75,000 to our expenses.

*Great! You would also need a GM, or general manager to run the day-to-day business for you. This would be an additional expense. A GM will probably not work for the $3,000 a month that you are paying yourselves right now. So we probably need to add another $50,000 - $75,000 for the GM.*

*If you add these additional expenses to your total revenue we calculated earlier as your revenue target for exiting your business.*

**Required Total Revenue + (New Employees + New Equipment) + (GM) = Required Total Revenue**

**$240,000 + $75,000 + $75,000 = $390,000**

Hmmm, $390,000 in annual revenue is within our reach. We've never had the business that big before. But if we put the right systems and people in place I think that we could do it.

*It sounds like you have found your motivation to grow ECC the right way!*

So how do we get there?

*It's actually simpler than you might think.*

## Learn how to be a business owner and not just a business worker.

You've probably heard the cliché "stop working *in* your business, and start working *on* your business." And here's what that means: As a business owner, you need to focus more on *thinking* about the strategic objectives necessary to drive your business than on the actual doing.

Remember, business self-sustainability is the goal. You need to reduce the time that you spend worrying about and doing day-to-day tasks to bring sales and revenue in the door.

The problem is many small business owners don't know what they need to do to work *on* their business.

## The 3 skills of business self-sustainability

To create self-sustainability, you need to learn how to do three things:

> 1. Understand what factors drive your business and how to measure them.
>
> 2. Create systems using the measures to create consistent, predictable revenue and profit.
>
> 3. Delegate responsibility and control to others.

Sounds easy enough — right? Well, it might be and it might not be, depending on whether you have the same bad habits that keep most small business owners from doing what they need to do.

The most difficult part of achieving self-sustainability isn't learning these new skills. It's *unlearning the bad habits* you have developed along the way. Let's take a look at how to implement and master these three skills.

*Understand what drives your business and how to measure it*

Becoming a true business owner is just learning how to systematically manage your business. Our management model, "Tuning Your Revenue Engine," or something like it to predictively understand the causes and effects of your operation so you can monitor and manage your cash flow is an example of systematic managing your business.

By understanding causes and effects in your business, you can see what most likely will happen when you make certain decisions. As a result you make better decisions.

*Our owners' business drivers*

*Mike, I think you have something like this — a way to understand and measure your business drivers — for Mega Power, don't you?*

Absolutely!

*What things are important to your business and what do you measure and monitor them?*

Each morning I run a report telling me exactly what's going on in Mega Power. It's a one-page summary with seven items:

1. How much cash does the company have on-hand?

2. How much in accounts receivable — A/R — does the company have?

3. How much in accounts payable — A/P — does the company have?

4. How many units are in production and being shipped in the next week?

5. How many sales have closed to date for the month?

6. How many deals are being worked by the sales team?

7. How many new leads have come in to date for the month?

*That's a pretty powerful dashboard. I can see many of these measures being important to most companies. But there may be slightly different metrics that are needed for other businesses like yours, Chris and Ann. Do you know what these values are for your business?*

Wow, we could do a lot if we knew this stuff for our business! It would probably be important for us to know how many jobs we had for the day, week, and month. But we'd need to set up better reporting systems than we have right now.

*Good point, Chris and Ann. You're beginning to see the importance of systems, aren't you?*

Yes we do.

*Well then let's take a look at what you need to do to create reporting systems.*

### Create systems for consistent, predictable revenue and profits

You've read about systems several times to this point. To reiterate, systems are nothing more than documenting what you're doing (procedures), then making sure everyone is following those procedures when they accomplish those tasks within the business. Read the section titled "5 Steps to formalizing your business systems" in an earlier part of this book if you are unsure what to do here.

It's this skill —creating systems that give you consistent predictability — where many business owners struggle most. It's all about getting people to follow the procedures. This means creating performance-based accountability for everyone in the business, and then following through with regular reviews and evaluations to assure accountability.

If you figured out your performance measures for your business drivers, then your next step is to apply those measures to your operation. First, you want to figure out where each of these measures should be running and set a target or baseline. Next, you need to publish these targets as the standard for the company. Once you've done this you can begin evaluating each person's performance against the standards. If they are meeting the standard then everything is good.

If people underperform compared to the standard, then you need to decide how you'll handle it. Do you train and develop people? Or, do you put underperformers on probation or fire them?

If people outperform their target, things are great! So how do you motivate people to seek to achieve this outcome? You can use bonuses, awards, vacations, recognition, and so on.

There are plenty of ways to motivate people. Once you have goals so people know the expectation, it's easier for them to perform as desired. And, it's easier for you to develop reward systems to motivate people. All of this is at the core of creating accountability throughout your business.

*How our owners create consistent, predictable systems*

*Mike you seem to have this well-in-hand at Mega Power.*

Yes, what you described here is pretty much what we follow with our 43 employees. It works very well. And because it's so objective, instead of subjective, employees take a fraction of the time it takes many other business owners who I know around town.

*How about you, Chris and Ann?*

We are still working on it. The checklist that you suggested earlier is one of nearly a dozen different procedures that we need to put in place. One of those procedures is developing a dashboard similar to what Mike has for his business. Once we have that, I think we can begin really paying our techs for their performance with bonuses. We see how that would motivate them to do an even better job.

*So you see how those key metrics are the first step?*

Absolutely! This is something that we always wanted to do. We just didn't know what to measure and how to measure it. Now that we are learning how to make proactive decisions from information instead of just reacting when a crisis occurs, we will be in much better shape.

I am already beginning to feel a calm I cannot remember ever having. Weirdly, it also makes me a little uneasy!

*Actually Ann, this uneasy feeling means that you're changing. Changing yourselves is what you need to do to make the changes in your business necessary to get to business self-sustainability.*

### Delegate responsibility and control to others

Finally, you need to build a team to help you. Once your systems are built and creating the results you want, getting others to do the work is much easier. This is what delegation is all about.

Most owners have a difficult time delegating for two reasons. The first one— not knowing what to delegate or how to know if it's being doing right — is easy to solve. You understand and measure what drives your business, and you create systems that use those measures to create consistent, predictable revenue and profit. Now you can easily delegate work and have a high level of confidence that you will get the results you want.

The second reason delegating is a challenge is that it's a mental/emotional hurdle. Here is that psychological thing again! Owners often struggle with giving up control of their business. Again, it's because they are too emotionally attached to it.

Believe me, I get it. You put a lot of hard work, blood, sweat, and tears to get it here! However, to get your business where you really want it, you have to change the way you think about and behave with it!

This is why the first step of the SPARC process is to define your passion. You are more likely to change if you understand what you really want out of life.

Once you know what you want out of life, you just use your business as a vehicle to get you there. If you think of your business as a vehicle to achieve your desires, it will be much easier to let go.

### How do our owners deal with delegation?

*Chris and Ann, you two seem to know what you want. But can you delegate, delegate, delegate to get there?*

Yes, we want to be able spend time raising our children. And, we have never done anything else except clean carpets. We'd like to go and experience life and share it with our kids while they're still young. Building ECC into a self-sustaining business gives us the independence and financial freedom to do that. We don't have our egos tied to our business, so that's not holding us back on delegating more. Our real issues truly understanding and measuring our business drivers so we can develop repeatable systems.

*Wow, this is very perceptive and you have this honed into a very specific goal and why it's important. Good job! How about you Mike?*

I see that even though Mega Power is a great business, I've been managing it as a lifestyle business. My family and I have everything we want. And, I know how hard it was to get it. Now, I may be afraid to lose it by handing it to someone else. But I have to or I'll never be free. And, my family is at risk should something unexpected happen to me.

*Mike, thanks for sharing this revelation with us. It takes a lot of courage to admit what you just admitted. Would you be willing to share what helped you realize what you just shared?*

Yea, my handling of the project with Bill and his team! I had to ask myself what would make me act that way?

I know that what I really want is spending time with Cathy, my children, and grandchildren. So why was being on the leading edge so important to me? It's my competitive nature. I had it when I started in sales more than 30 years ago; I used it to grow Mega Power; and it still drives me today.

*That's very insightful. Do you think that you can push past it if it's been a part of you for that long?*

Yes, I know I can. Now that I realize that my competitiveness is what drives me, I can use it to achieve my goal of getting Mega Power off my back so I can spend time with my family, like I want to.

*That is a great way to use a strength. Congratulations and good luck getting there.*

So see, to achieve business self-sustainability you need to become a better owner by:

- Understanding your metrics.
- Creating systems to generate consistent, predictable revenue.
- Building a team you can delegate work to.

## 4 Key sales objectives in the self-sustainability stage

Earlier, you learned how the sales function evolves as your business matures through the growth model. First, we looked at sales in the foundation stage, when your goal is to consistently break even; and then sales in the survival stage, when your goal is to consistently meet your profit requirement. Now, we want to look at how sales changes in the self-sustainability stage.

When your company gets to self-sustainability, like everything else in your business, you need to begin establishing and delegating sales processes so that others are doing the work. If you've followed the small business growth model to this point, then achieving self-sustainability is a fairly simple transition the next four things you need to do:

1. Implement your sales process.
2. Hire a sales team.
3. Train your team in your sales process.
4. Disengage from day-to-day selling.

If you haven't followed the model, then you'll need to return to the foundation or survival stages to complete unfinished work: establishing your sales process. If this is the case in your situation, then you need to go to the section titled "5 Critical Sales Actions in the Survival Stage" from earlier in this book to understand what you should already have done.

### Implement your sales process

If you followed completed the actions in the survival stage, then you should have a pretty good idea of what it takes to sell your products or services. The key is, it's written down so others can follow your recipe for sales success.

You may need to organize it, but that is the easy part. Usually all that knowledge about how to sell is locked in one or more heads: the owner, the sales reps, or both. It doesn't help the company there. The self-sustainability stage is all about making your business run by itself! Get your sales process out there so that others can generate sales for you.

### Hire a sales team

Once you have a sales manual or guide you're ready to begin hiring a sales team. The sales team is more than just hiring more reps. You need a sales manager too.

Many small business owners are usually okay hiring the reps. But they become terrified by the thought of hiring a manager! Usually this is because they fear losing control by delegating this part of their business to someone else.

The loss of control is really a fallacy. As a business owner, you actually have less control by not letting go. That's because you can only handle a finite amount of work by yourself. You become the chokepoint for sales in your own company. Again, you have to conquer the fear of letting go if you want true independence.

Often the fear stems from not understanding how to create the necessary management systems to manage the sales function and responsibility to the sales manager. Sales management is not as difficult as you might think, but it is not something that is taught in the classroom. It is usually learned in the trenches, so many owners don't know how to do it.

If you're using the "Tuning Your Revenue Engine" management model, then sales management is already part of your management system. DE, Inc. offers a program, "Selling by the Numbers," that demystifies the process of sales management by digging deeper into the sales portion of "Tuning Your Revenue Engine." You may want to check it out if sales management is still a sketchy area for you.

### Train your sales team to use your process

If you've implemented your process and begun hiring your sales team, then training your team is your obvious next step. This seems pretty straight forward. But again, if you didn't document things in the survival stage, then how do you train someone now?

A big failure for many small businesses is trying to use "on the job training" (OJT) to teach a sales rep. While you need to take a rep out on sales calls and get them familiar with your products or services, materials, and pitch, what happens when you send them out on their own?

They will only do those things that they remember. If they don't have scripts or checklists to follow, the chance that they will be successful is a crapshoot! By giving them the support tools they need to be successful, you increase their chances for giving you a successful return on investment.

*Disengage from day-to-day selling*

This is a hard one! In fact, a lot of owners tell me "I don't want to stop selling. I love it!" That's not the point. You must be able to disengage or you have not reached the self-sustainability stage of the growth model because your sales are attributed to you and require you for your top line to grow.

Remember, the self-sustainability stage has a major decision point — disengage or rapid growth. Even if you decide that you want rapid growth, you still will need to pass more and more selling off to others or your sales capacity will always be limited by what you can handle.

Another factor to consider is that capital will be a key resource in rapid growth. Capital will be hard to come by if you are a key component in your company's ability to scale top-line growth!

You can take on any role you chose as you move forward in your business as long as you can demonstrate two things.

1. Your business does not require you in that role to operate.

2. You have the necessary skills and experience to accomplish what must be accomplished in the next stage of the growth model.

## Ready. Set. *Sell!* How are our business owners faring?

*So there you have it. Your sales factors for achieving the self-sustainability stage of the small business growth model. Have you done what you needed prior to getting here? If not, what is your plan for completing unfinished business in your earlier stages?*

*Mike, it would appear that Mega Power has this one licked.*

Yes, while I do sell, I focus on big deals that help the bottom-line shoot to the moon! My VP of sales reminds me of myself 20 years ago. She is aggressive and keeps the team accountable to hitting their numbers. As a result, Mega Power is in a good position to move into the rapid growth stage. I just need to get out of my team's way.

*You're moving in the right direction. What about you, Ann and Chris'?*

A recent hire we made seems to have put us in a good position. Much is not currently documented; however I have delegated this to our new hire. So a sales guide is in the process of being developed.

Early indicators seem to point to the fact that he can sell. He and I closed several deals in the first few weeks and filled our sales funnel with new opportunities.

*Chris, I would say you are on the right track. Now, only time will tell if it's enough to get you to your overall sales goal or not.*

I would agree. Once we know this is moving in the right direction, then we want to focus more attention on the residential side of the business.

*This is a good plan. If you can have two different markets generating revenue you have spread your risk out. You are doing a great job of taking what you've learned and applying it.*

Thanks! That is helpful, knowing that we are on the right track.

## 2 Marketing objectives speed you through the self-sustainability stage

Before you can successfully market in the self-sustainability growth stage, you must decide what you are trying to accomplish next with your business. Are you planning to enter the rapid growth stage or will you be sustaining the company's current level of operation? Once you've decided what you plan to do with your business, your marketing objectives become clearer and so do your marketing tactics.

If your marketing objectives in the survival stage were successfully accomplished, you should be in good shape because two things are working for your marketing at this point:

1. Your marketing plan consistently delivers the leads needed to support sales.

2. Metrics allow you to monitor shifts in the market so that you can adapt as needed.

If these two things are on autopilot and do not require much of your attention, you can get through the self-sustainability stage quickly if you choose rapid growth. Or, if you choose just to sustain your current success, you can begin to disengage from your business.

## A solid marketing plan

This is a given. You won't have success if you don't have a solid marketing plan. Consistent profit comes from a consistent flow of business and that is generated with leads from marketing.

The key here is this: do others participate and manage your marketing plan or not? If it's all you, then you are still stuck in the survival stage. You need to begin to delegate more of your marketing if you want to get your business into the self-sustainability stage.

Many small businesses will outsource their marketing by hiring a marketing firm. This is a good approach, but make sure you hire a firm that can help you execute an integrated marketing strategy. Marketing is an ever changing landscape. If you outsource this function, your vendor needs to be your marketing director. This means they need to provide you with information you need to shift with the market.

## Monitoring your marketing

Again, this is a given. Metrics help you see what's going on. What's working and what's not. Use them to hone your marketing plan and get the right marketing mix. You want to maximize your revenue for the least marketing investment possible.

Another benefit of good monitoring is it tells you when something is going on in the economy or your market sector. As you see your marketing ratios begin to change ask "Why?" Companies that see increases or decreases in business coming adjust to meet the challenge. The ones that don't adjust struggle or die.

If you're monitoring and see a market shift that affects sales, then make the proper adjustment. Cut or add staff, expense, or both where it makes sense to get the results you want. It sounds easy because it is! The problem is most small businesses aren't tracking the right things to have this kind of visibility about their business. Look in the earlier part of this book for "3 Marketing Steps to Consistent Profits in the Survival Stage" if you are unclear on how to get the visibility you need to be successful with your marketing and business.

## Marketing with our owners

*Chris and Ann, marketing seems to be an issue with you. What seems to be the problem?*

We're just stumped. We don't think that we have ever really done that much marketing.

*I disagree. If you haven't then you wouldn't have a business. You just don't realize what marketing is. You seem to think that marketing equals advertising. While advertising is one form of promotion, it is only one of many. And while advertising is OK for some businesses, it may not be right for your business. The problem is without tracking what you've done in the past you have no way of knowing.*

You're right. We've started tracking and see that a certain level of calling and visiting properties during the week has created a couple of new accounts and several others that we expect to close in the next six months.

*Well, guess what? This is marketing!*

*So for the commercial part of your business this is the marketing plan. And as you determine how many calls and visits create a sale, you have the formula for the commercial division of your business.*

Yes, that would let us monitor what is going on and what we need to do more of. If we had this in place we could had this off to Matt, our new general manager, and Chris could focus on the residential sales.

*That's exactly right. However, the residential side of the business is a different animal all together. As you tracked the few calls that you got over the month from homeowners, your found that almost all are finding you on the web.*

*This makes sense as you have no other advertising or consumer-based marketing. So if you do nothing at all, you get between five and seven residential calls.*

*Now you can begin adding other tactics to your marketing mix to see how they influence the numbers and make adjustments or add more dollars to your marketing budget to get the level of sales to create the revenue necessary to support your business self-sustainability goal.*

I see that. We just need to keep doing what we're doing and add to it as we see what's working and what's not.

*Exactly! You owners are on fire. Let's see what you need to do with the operation now.*

## 2 Operational Goals Help You Stop Working at Self-Sustainability

As you now know, there is a decision you make about which of two paths to take after you achieve the self-sustainability stage. The first path is to step away from your business and let it sustain your current lifestyle. If this is your path, then you need to be able to say "Yes" to two questions:

1. Does my business create self-sustaining cash flow?

2. What is my business succession or exit plan?

The second path is to enter the rapid growth stage and grow your business into a big corporation. If this is your plan, then you still need to have a self-sustaining cash flow. Your business succession or exit plan, however, can wait.

The curious thing is no matter which path you choose, how your business operates at this stage is the same! You only need ask one question — your litmus test — to determine if you have achieved the self-sustainability stage or not:

*Does my business create self-sustaining cash flow?*

If your answer is "No," then you haven't yet achieved the self-sustainability stage of the growth model. You still have work to do in this stage or earlier stages.

If your goal is self-sustainability, then your next step is planning whether you'll pass your business to someone else or to sell it.

If you plan to enter the rapid growth stage, you next step is to understand even more deeply your revenue engine metrics. Your metrics will tell you the cause and effect of your business, so that you know what operational decisions to make going forward.

For example, if you increase your sales plan by X, how many additional orders can you expect? Now, you can plan appropriately in operations as you begin to turn up the sales flow so that your operation can handle the increased volume of new orders. There will be other things to address in the rapid growth stage; we'll look at that in the next chapter.

*Does my business create self-sustaining cash flow?*

If you completed all the foundation stage requirements for marketing, sales, and operations, then those departments will be creating breakeven cash flow month after month without you even thinking about it. If you applied the same principles to the requirements in the survival stage then — instead of merely breaking even — you are creating a very nice profit month-to-month.

So why are the foundation and survival stages so important in a section about self-sustainability stage operations? Because the things recommended in the foundation and survival stages are critical to self-sustainable business operations. Yet lack of self-sustainable operations is what most frequently prevents owners from having a self-sustainable business and is what most small business owners will think they can do without and avoid along the way.

Many small business owners say, "The foundation and survival stages are too early to be thinking about this stuff." So when these naysayers get to what they believe to be the self-sustainability stage, they cannot step away from their business because they're stuck in "nowhere land".

Their business just stalls. They do nothing about it until they absolutely have to, and then discover it will take three to five years to do what they should have been doing all along. The problem is at that point they just want to be done with it. The result is many lose out on a lot of money and don't achieve the success they dreamed of when they started their business.

If you're not sure of the operational requirements of the foundation and survival stages, go back to the earlier part of this book and re-read these sections:

- 4 Operational Objectives in the Foundation Stage
- How to Profitably Refine Your Operation in the Survival Stage

If you accomplished what was recommended in those sections, then in self-sustainability your operation actions are just monitoring, and maintaining equipment and assets used in production. If your goal is to keep growing your business, then you will also add capacity as needed to support your business's growth.

*Where are our owners operationally?*

*So Brandy, where are you operationally?*

I haven't even started so you can move on from me.

*Well, that's not entirely true. If you have determined what you are going to sell then you need to think about how you're going to deliver it. So you need to have some idea.*

I guess you're right. But since you made the case for starting my business by selling consulting services, this sort of changes my entire operational model. So I really need to give this some thought.

*I would agree with you there. At least you realize that you need to think it through.*

*What about you two, Chris and Ann, where are you?*

Well, we are still very actively engaged in our monthly cash flow. But we are working on it. If you look at some of the objectives that we have been working on since learning about the stages of the growth model, we have seen a distinctive shift.

Our actions are helping us to delegate more and more to others in the company. Systems are a major focus as we tackle each new objective. I think it's only a matter of time before we are at the self-sustainability stage. In fact, I can see us achieving our overall revenue goal in the next 12 to 18 months, and not three years like we had initially planned.

*That's great! Do you have your cruise booked yet?*

Not yet, but we're thinking about when would be the best time of year to go!

*What about you, Mike?*

I think our business indicates that we are mostly self-sustainable and can stay here if we want to. I just need to let go of my decision making responsibility! I need to talk to Bill today about our production project. And, I really need to begin looking at a succession or exit plan.

*Hey now there is a good topic - succession or exit planning. Let's take a look at these very critical aspects of successful business growth.*

### Succession or exit planning - Which one should you use?

Disengaging from your business, if you chose to stay in self-sustainability, requires a certain set of actions. These actions are transferring your responsibilities to someone else. This is really what the term business succession means. But succession planning is not exit planning.

Often the terms succession planning and exit planning get used interchangeably. However, there is a definitive difference between the two. It's important that you understand the difference:

- *Succession planning* focuses on transferring the *power or leadership* of a business.
- *Exit planning* focuses on transferring the *wealth and ownership* of a business.

*Succession planning* is really identifying, training, and transferring the leadership and management of a business to another person or team of people. Exit planning, on the other hand, is identifying and executing the transfer strategy of a company and its ownership to another person, team, or entity.

Succession planning is almost always a part of exit planning. However, when done correctly, exit planning doesn't have to end, as most owners believe, with the sale of their business. And succession planning can add huge value to your business. Let me explain what I mean.

### Succession planning without exit planning

For years now, I have advocated creating a self-sustaining business. What this really means is building your business in a way where it runs itself. Or at least in a way that doesn't require you to be there to assure that it generates the level of cash flow and profit that you want.

If your goal is to create a self-sustaining small business (not a big corporation), then succession planning is your final business growth stage, and your next step is finding that person to take on the day-to-day role you play running your business so that you can go off and do other things. Like playing with that folder full of ideas you've been saving because you finally learned how to control your shiny-object syndrome.

*Exit planning doesn't have to mean sell my business!*

If your business is set up to be self-sustaining, it just becomes another investment in your portfolio. Just like your mutual funds in your 401K or other retirement investments, your business's cash flow generates the money for your retirement.

Now, this approach is not for everyone. Some people will say, "I don't want to mess with it. When I am ready to retire then I want to sell my business and be done with it."

That's OK, too! But there is one other thing to consider. Even if selling your business is your exit strategy, your business will have more value, and more buyers will be interested if your business already has someone else managing it! That's because you've already taken care of your succession plan.

*Succession planning adds values when exit planning*

The fantasy too many small business owners live is that they'll find someone who can afford to pay them the $1 million or more that the owners *think* their businesses are worth. Wrong!

According to business broker statistics, fewer than 25% of businesses that go on the market are actually sold. Can you afford to leave your retirement to those odds?

People with that kind of money — $1 million or more — *don't run businesses*. They buy businesses that somebody else runs for them! So if your business isn't self-sustaining, then you'll be the one running it if an investor buys it.

A buyer will pay you more if your business already has a general manager in place to run it! They will pay you much less if they have to find a manager, train the manager, and then transfer the management responsibility to the manager. In fact, they'll probably require that you stay on and find, train, and transition the new manager as part of the deal. If you cannot make that transition, you'll be stuck with your business again, have a legal battle on your hands, and have wasted a year or more of your life and retirement in the process!

So if you plan your succession before you sell, you'll get more when you do sell. Remember:

*Succession Planning = $$$$!*

Succession planning is always part of building a business. Exit planning, however, really depends on how and to whom you plan to transfer the ownership of your business. Make sure you have a succession plan that you are working on when you first enter the self-sustainability stage of growth; don't put it off.

*How are our company owners handling their exit plans?*

*Let's start with you again, Brandy.*

It's too early for me to be thinking about exit planning.

*You are wrong. Every business owner must consider this early in the business's life as it can influence how you build the business. Let me explain what I mean.*

*Brandy, let's say that your initial thought is that you'd like to sell your software solution at some point in the future to a big software company. Then you need to understand what type companies might be interested and look at what things are important to those companies. Then you would make those requirements part of your business plan so that you includes them in the process of building and growing your company. So an exit strategy is critical when you start your business.*

OK, that make sense.

*Ann and Chris, you two have already made your decision, right?.*

Yup, we want to keep the business, but we want it to run itself. Then we can go off and do something else. Maybe build another business in another industry and another location in the country.

*I like the way that you two are starting to dream. This is giving you even more motivation to do what you need to do!*

We love the idea of business self-sustainability! It is an idea that nobody in our circle of trusted advisors ever discussed with us.

*That doesn't surprise me. Most trusted advisors make a boatload of cash when they help sell a business. So they want you to sell your business, even if it's not in your best interest financially!*

*What about you, Mike?*

I am frustrated! My frustration comes from seeing how much of my own ego has been wrapped up in my role as a CEO and I haven't been really acting like a business owner.

*Well, don't beat yourself up so much. You understand where you are now and you can do something about it. So what do you think you're going to do, exit or succession?*

I'm not going to sell the business. I'm going to keep it as part of our estate. I'm going to begin working to transfer president and CEO responsibility to someone on my executive team and then I'll become the chairman of the board for the company.

I'll have an owners meeting at least quarterly or maybe even monthly. In these meetings I will lay out major directional decisions for my senior management team and they can report progress on past decisions. This will allow me to influence decisions that might put my family's financial security in jeopardy. But I will stay out of all the senior executives' daily decisions.

*That's a very solid game plan. I don't think that I would have advised you any differently. Can you see how this helps you run a business from a distance? It's just another system that you need to put in place.*

*Reports, which you should already be preparing, get generated. You compare what you planned to do and see where you are tracking and ended up. Then you make any corrections necessary or turn up the heat on providing service because your sales far exceeded your expectations.*

I think this will work. Cathy will be excited to see that there is a light at the end of the tunnel!

*I believe she will have a smile on her face after that conversation.*

## Chapter 12: Rapid Growth Stage Strategy

If you get to this stage - rapid growth, it's because you set the goal to grow your business in the self-sustainability stage. But be careful; while many business owners consciously say they want to grow their small businesses into large ones, in their hearts they don't really have the desire to do what it takes. Why? Because leaving corporate America is the reason many owners started their small businesses in the first place! Assuming rapid growth is what you want, then know your goal at this point.

*Goal: Assure that growth does not outpace assets,*

*resources, and systems.*

In the rapid growth stage, large sums of capital are needed as the business takes on more and more customers thus needing more equipment and materials. Also, the number of employees to service these new customers seems ever expanding. Properly managed, rapid growth turns small businesses into big companies. If not properly managed, this stage can be the death of your company.

As with the other stages, rapid growth has its own challenges and risks an owner must manage. If they don't, then any one of these things can consume and destroy the company:

- High demand for cash creates a high debt-equity ratio that makes it difficult to get credit lines.

- Lacking cash, credit, or both can cause the business to seek equilibrium by reverting to an earlier stage, or worse by going under.

- Moving into unrelated businesses can be disastrous because it strips critical resource needed for growth.

- The CEO tries to save money by not hiring people or by laying them off, and therefore risks losing the company because there aren't enough people to keep the company growing.

You can see where rapid growth can quickly become an albatross for someone without a love for business.

If you choose the rapid growth path, then here are the aspects of the leadership and management factors you should focus on.

| Leadership Factors | Focus in Rapid Growth Stage |
|---|---|
| *Owner Goals* | • Commit to a growth strategy for the business<br>• Choose your role: none (disengaged) or advisory |
| *Operational Skills* | • Not applicable |
| *Managerial Abilities* | • Not applicable |
| *Strategic Thinking* | • Include managers in planning strategies |

| Management Factors | Focus in Rapid Growth Stage |
|---|---|
| *Financial Assets* | • Use a profitability-planning system<br>• Assure adequate financing to keep pace with growth<br>• Manage cash flow with expense and budget controls<br>Money sources: Continue with earlier sources and add...<br>• Joint ventures<br>• Banks<br>• Licensing<br>• New investors<br>• Partners |
| *Personnel Resources* | • Expand a skilled, experienced and competent management structure |
| *Systems* | • Refine and extend systems to keep pace with growth<br>• Fine-tune management systems<br>• Use systems to do financial planning, forecasting, and to model growth strategies |
| *Business Assets* | • Add tangible and intangible assets to aid growth |

As you move into the rapid growth stage focus within the eight growth factors becomes much more formalized as the MBA's move in. Here are nine main objectives within the 8 growth factors where structure and systems will be add to every aspect of your business:

1. Financing rapid growth.

2. Owner delegation to improve managerial effectiveness.

3. Decentralized organizational managers must be extremely competent.

4. Talented managers and key employees.

5. Company systems must be tested, altered and delegated, with strong strategic leadership from top management.

6. Marketing focuses on moving into new markets.

7. Partner with businesses complementing existing experience and capabilities.

8. New products or services are added to existing markets.

9. Existing business is expanded into new markets and customer types.

If you plan to successfully jump to the rapid growth stage, there are five owner accomplishments you need to be able to claim — but are often lacking in books written on rapid growth. Make sure you're prepared before you make the leap.

## 5 Owner accomplishments required for rapid business growth

There are dozens of articles and blog posts written every day about what you need to really grow a business. Most tout the most obvious aspect — more money and financing; better marketing; added sales; raving customers; and so on. In other words, exactly the same things you need for a successful business of any size! But what are the subtle things that really improve your chances of rapid growth success? What are the owner accomplishments separating the super successful businesses from just the average ones?

One of my past clients called me to help them out as they were getting frighteningly close to the point of *out of control*. It caused me to look closely at the subtle things that separate the *big* from the privately owned businesses. And what I discovered are five accomplishments that really stick out for owners who successfully jump to rapid growth:

1. Clear vision of the future

2. Master of delegation

3. Solid key metrics for monitoring all aspects of the business

4. Development of a senior management team

5. Solid and scalable processes and systems

### *Clear vision of the future*

Creating a clear vision is both an owner competency and accomplishment because it's the litmus test for every business decision. If a clear vision isn't defined, managers as well as employees don't have any idea whether they are making the right decisions for the company or not.

The result is one of two possibilities.

1. You spend time and resources undoing the wrong decisions.

2. Nobody is willing to make a decision and you waste valuable time as an owner answering questions every day that could easily be handled by others.

### *Master of delegation*

Delegation is also both a competency and an accomplishment because it means communicating to others and letting go! As noted earlier, many owners struggle with delegation. Add the lack of a clear vision for the future, and delegation becomes ten times harder.

Delegating is more than just handing out tasks to others. That's just doling out assignments. Delegating is all about:

- Setting a direction.

- Setting standards for quality.

- Defining the performance parameters to measure success.

- Holding people accountable for successfully achieving the desired quality standards.

Most people just give a very simple assignment with no parameters and then wonder why they don't get the result they expected. It's because they never set the expectation in the beginning about how success would be measured.

### Solid key metrics for monitoring all aspects of the business

As a business owner, if you don't know the causes and effects of operations on revenue, you're dead before you start. It's not as hard to figure out as you might think. Once again, the "Tuning Your Revenue Engine" model can help you determine the key metrics by which to manage your business.

The formulas you figured out earlier in the growth model will change over time. For example, as you speed up rapid growth your revenue formula may change. You will no doubt look for ways to streamline your operations and squeeze more out of every resource. As you do, your baseline metrics will change. Just make sure when your metrics change to also update your formulas.

### Development of a senior management team

You, as a business owner, cannot face rapid growth alone. Remember that your primary goal during the rapid growth stage is to assure that growth does not outpace assets, resources, and systems. This takes competent senior managers at the helm of every department or function.

Without a senior management team, *you* become the limiting factor in your business. This reduces the value of your business because you are not scalable.

True business investors look for businesses with strong teams because it spreads risk and gives them confidence that the business can survive the loss of one of the key personnel. Having strong teams should give you the same kind of confidence.

### Solid and scalable processes and systems

Finally, processes and systems are a must! If you can't quickly and easily train someone to do a job in your business, it will slow you down.

During rapid growth, one of the biggest challenges is always ramping up staff. Again, investors understand this and that's why they want to buy companies that have cash flow created by solid systems. This gives the business self-sustainability. Investors love that.

You can easily find 100 other things that are necessary for rapid growth. But when a company is stuck, then it's usually because the owner hasn't accomplished the five things needed for rapid growth: vision for the future, delegation, key metrics, a senior management team, and scalable processes and systems.

Remember the client who called me because they were close to being out of control during rapid growth? Here's the funny thing: although they listened well in their earlier stages, they developed some hearing loss somewhere between self-sustainability and rapid growth. At least in part, they stopped listening because they felt uneasy, maybe even scared, about moving from small to big. Now that they're refocused on the five accomplishments to reach the rapid growth goal — don't outpace your resources — their hearing is greatly improved.

## 3 Critical sales objectives for rapid growth

The rapid growth stage is all about becoming a big business and is not for the faint of heart. You have to be brave to reach the three sales objectives of rapid growth:

1. Expand your market

2. Do not outsell your delivery capacity

3. Hire, hire, hire!

*Are you ready to scale your sales?*

Before you can "turn the faucet on full flow!" you should audit your business to be sure you've met the critical sales objectives from earlier stages. Here's a quick review:

*Stage 1 - Foundation: 3 Critical sales questions you must answer*

1. How many sales does it take to break even?

2. Who buys what you sell?

3. How do you reach them?

*Stage 2 - Survival: 5 Critical sales actions*

1. Document your sales process

2. Validate your market research

3. Determine your conversion rate

4. Learn about and develop ways to overcome objections

5. Use customer input to improve your pitch

*Stage 3 - Self-Sustainability: 4 key sales actions*

1. Implement your sales process

2. Hire a sales team

3. Train your sales team to use your process

4. Disengage from day-to-day selling

If your audit shows you've met those objectives, then you're ready to expand, outsell, and hire.

### Implement market expansion

The first job of your sales team is to implement the market expansion plan. Your senior management team set the market expansion goals, and your marketing team created a plan for raising consumer awareness. Now it's the job of your sales team to find and sell to consumers who are shopping for your products or services.

Sales must also work closely with marketing by providing the "real world" feedback to marketing. Marketing, in turn, needs to confirm or adjust the assumptions in the marketing strategy and plan so Sales can do their job. .

### Do not outsell your capacity

Rapid growth is a balancing act! That is, sales cannot outsell the company's capacity to produce. If it does then sales creates an even bigger problem for the business.

The systems put in place in the self-sustainability stage must be used here to understand how much new business the production department can handle. It is the sales department's job to maximize sales resources in filling that production capacity.

How do you do this? Again this is a great place for the "Tuning Your Revenue Engine" model. Keep these performance numbers at your fingertips and continue to monitor operational capacity.

### Hire, hire, hire!

If you have excess capacity, then you need a big enough sales team to sell it all. And that might mean you have to hire more sales people.

Hiring more sales people is probably the one objective that prevents most small businesses from rapid growth. If you haven't been a sales VP in a large company, the necessary skills may feel a little foreign to you. This is where hiring a sales executive becomes critical.

Another critical person will be a HR director. There are many administrative actions necessary in the hiring process. You need a seasoned HR professional to manage recruiting, hiring, retaining, and letting go of employees or you need to outsource it to an organization like a PEO (professional employer organization).

So there you have it. Is your sales department ready to deal with the rapid growth stage challenges? Get your ducks in a row, or this stage can be even more difficult than the early ones.

*Is rapid growth what you really want?*

If you're not feeling real comfortable, then your gut is trying to tell you something. Maybe the rapid growth stage is not really for you. If not, you may want to begin developing an exit strategy more in tune with your desired outcome. If you're not sure what to do, you should begin talking to your trusted advisors like your CPA, financial planner, executive advisor/mentor, insurance agent, lawyer, etc. for assistance. This is a big decision. Make sure you get all the facts before you head down this path.

## Checking in with our owners

*So let me start with you, Mike. Is rapid growth in the cards for Mega Power?*

You know it was, but I won't be a part of it.

*Why do you say that?*

Well, if I do it then how am I going to do what Cathy and I want to do?

*Delegate!*

Delegate? Delegate the growth?

*Exactly! Why couldn't you let the team you've assembled do it?*

I guess I can. I just never thought about it that way. I always thought I'd lead that effort.

*Hey, look at it this way. If you get what you and Cathy want — time with the kids and you not endlessly hung up with the business — then do you really care how big the team grows the company? You just reap the rewards of their actions!*

I like the way that sounds!

*What about you, Chris and Ann?*

We were just discussing that. This may be a way for us to share ownership with our employees. If they grow it way beyond what we need or want, then we'd be willing to give them a stake in what they've accomplished.

*I like the way you two are thinking. This is exactly what I have always recommended to my clients. Why not share with those key employees in a way that makes it nearly impossible for them to leave. Ownership is definitely one of those strategies.*

## Chapter 13: Maturity Stage Strategy

So here we are at the end of the model, in the maturity stage. You might think that, if properly managed, maturity is the end of your business growth. But if you remember the goal of maturity, you realize that it's not the end.

*Goal: To diversify the company by offering related products or services to existing customers or by entering new markets.*

The key question is, does your business mature with or without you? If the latter, then you'll attend to those aspects of leadership and management that help you completely disengage. Maybe you have legal documents to sign, farewell letters to write, and a party to plan.

But if you decide to stay involved, then your role in the maturity stage is to be an advisor. Your leadership and management focus switches to advising your executive team on how to diversify the business.

| Leadership Factors | Focus in Maturity Stage |
|---|---|
| *Owner Goals* | • Be an advisor, period |
| *Operational Skills* | • Participate in executive meetings where decisions are made about changes in growth or changes in systems |
| *Managerial Abilities* | • Advise your executive team on how to manage diversification of the business |
| *Strategic Thinking* | • Watch for new markets, products, or services for growing the business |

| Management Factors | Focus in Maturity Stage |
| --- | --- |
| *Financial Assets* | • Consolidate and control financial gains from rapid growth stage |
| *Personnel Resources* | • Bring on a board of directors (BoD)<br>• Advise the BoD on developing a diversification plan |
| *Systems* | • Aid the planning of strategies, budgets, and operations for the purpose of diversification<br>• Build and documented to manage risk while retaining the flexibility of entrepreneurship<br>• Align with management with business objectives |
| *Business Assets* | • Add significant tangible and intangible business assets to the balance sheet |

## Wait for maturity to tackle maturity objectives

Many small business owners get stuck in earlier stages because they "jump the gun" and, wittingly or not, they try to operate as a mature business while still figuring their way out of an earlier stage. Offering new products and services is fine when you have 10,000 customers and consistent profitability. But when you're still in the survival (or for any other earlier) stage then, diversification is a *distraction*!

Assuming your business is in maturity, then your senior executives will do two things to diversify; they'll

1. decide which new products or services to offer

2. create a new business unit to create or find, and then sell the new offerings

In other words, the new product or service line becomes a new business. And that means the new business unit is in which stage? That's right, it's in the foundation stage.

Do you see what happens here? Diversifying your offering is just like opening a new company!

The problem when you try to diversify in earlier stages is you haven't mastered the skills you need to be self-sustainable with even your first product line! What makes you think that you'll have success by starting a second business at this point?

Listen, I get it. I've had the entrepreneur fever since I was 12 years old! Most of us are wired a little different and have a hard time focusing on one opportunity. But if you want to have success, you have to conquer shiny object syndrome.

Your shiny object syndrome is flaring up every time you get another great idea. If you are disciplined, then you learn to quickly evaluate the opportunity and decide if you should chase it or not.

Many small business owners are not well disciplined. And they spend months or even years chasing after the shiny object, they find themselves in a rabbit hole, having wasted time, money, and resources on something that cannot help them actually grow their existing business.

## Checking in with our owners

*So Brandy, do you think what we're talking about here applies to your situation?*

Why are you asking? How does this apply to me? I am just getting started. So I am in the foundation stage.

*That's a very good question. But much of what is necessary in the maturity stage is the same as when you're starting a business.*

*Let me show you what I mean. You are thinking of starting a business and quitting your job, right?*

Yes, that's what I am thinking of doing. But I'm not sure yet. I still have a lot of things to evaluate and need to see if it's in my best interest.

*Exactly! That is what companies do in the maturity stage or whenever they are evaluating a new idea. Whether it's a new product, service, market segment, or something else. They need to evaluate and decide if it meets their business goals and objectives. Just like you are doing in the beginning of your business!*

When you put it that way, I see the similarities.

*Great. This is why it's important to master the skills you need in the earlier stages of your business's growth; so you'll know how to grow each new product or service as the new small business that it is.*

You know, I have seen that at Mega Power too.

*What do you mean, Mike?*

If I had mastered the delegation skills earlier, then I would be out of my business and fishing on my boat!

*That's very perceptive. I am glad that both of you are seeing how each stage connects with another.*

## 5 Questions help you get past shiny object syndrome

Small business owners get distracted from their main vision all the time. It's amazing how many owners have attention deficit disorder (ADD).

ADD can be a strength in business. But it also presents challenges by creating shiny object syndrome!

Shiny object syndrome stems from a person's ability to see opportunity in new ideas. Seeing the upside is a must in becoming a successful entrepreneur. But so is *tempering* that with an ability to look at the downside.

Here are five questions you need to answer whenever you see a shiny object:

1. How does this idea fit into my vision?

2. Does it accelerate the timeline to self-sustainability for a current product or service line?

3. Does this idea increase the revenue and profitability of my current business?

4. How does this idea change my current systems?

5. How much overhead does this idea add to my current operation?

### How does this idea fit into my vision?

This is the first question you must ask yourself in evaluating a new idea. If it doesn't fit into your current business vision, put it in a file for later!

If your idea doesn't directly help you attain your vision, then it will hinder by distracting you from what you must focus on for success. If the idea makes sense then ask the next question, if not then leave it as a hobby for your retirement!

*Does it accelerate the timeline to self-sustainability for a current product or service line?*

If the idea doesn't help you get where you're trying to go faster, then what is the point? Time is money. So if your new idea delays achieving self-sustainability in another area, there had better be a good reason.

If the idea really does get you where you're trying to go faster, then great! You can ask the next question.

*Does this idea increase the revenue and profitability of my current business?*

Ok, let's ask the money question! Can you make money with this idea or not? Much of your evaluation should focus on market analysis. It doesn't matter if the idea looks good in a spreadsheet. Will anybody really buy it? And will they buy it for the price you have in your spreadsheet?

If you're trying to get investors interested and they're not, that should tell you something. Maybe there's something you've overlooked or missed, or maybe there's no real "there" there.

For example, because she's managed a training-systems project, Brandy already knows what's out there and has experience in finding a feasible solution. As with many "wantrapreneurs," Brandy believes lots of other companies want and will pay for a training system solution. She needs to test her theory. This is a good idea anyway, as she may be able to find other companies willing to help her fund her startup to get the system she is thinking about. By testing her theory, Brandy has a much higher chance of success and less risk than by just winging it. The problem is many inventors and "wantrapreneurs" want their shiny object so bad they're afraid of finding out they're wrong. So they skip the upfront research, and later regret losing time and money because they misjudged the market.

*How does this opportunity change my current systems?*

Adding up all this new work for your new idea — build it, sell it, deliver it; bill and collect for it, and (most importantly!) to service and support it — should make you pause. Where will you find the time and resources to implement your idea?

Continuing with Brandy as our example, she knows she'll be spending all her spare time on her new business. She isn't married and doesn't have kids, so that's not a problem. But she does have a boyfriend;

will he stick around if Brandy doesn't have time for him? More than one relationship has been destroyed by a starting a new business, so she needs to know.

Additionally, at some point she will quit her job. What kind of effect will that have on her life? It will definitely impact her personal cash flow. This is the same kind of problem many business owners face when they decide to go into new markets or add new products and services. Make sure you understand the overall impact on your life and business, and that you have the money before you move forward.

*How much overhead does this idea add to my current operation?*

If you have answers to the last question, then you're ready to add all the costs and additional resources to your current business budget and see how it changes your current financial position. This is how investors think through an opportunity, by evaluating the ROI. Stealing money from your other lines of business to make your new idea happen is never a good strategy. So if you do your homework, you will have a better chance of funding your new ideas.

Are you prone to shiny object syndrome? Then save time and money by evaluating your new ideas with the above questions. While money is often the motivation, your time is your most precious resource in every stage of the growth model. Protect it!

## Can our owners get past shiny object syndrome?

*Ok, although no one is rapid growth, let alone maturity, you've learned that, once you get there, you stay there by repeating the same stages for every new market or business line, and by avoiding shiny object syndrome.*

*So now let's end at the start. How about if we apply this your situation, Brandy. You're thinking of taking a whole new career path. Your shiny object for your business is a new training platform. While exciting, you still need to answer the first question: does it really help you meet your personal vision?*

I think so. I think I have something to sell that people will pay for.

*I get that, but does it align with what you really want out of life? Does the idea of developing a new training platform help you achieve your life's ambition? If it does then you can move on to the next question.*

*In your case, Brandy, you currently seem to be on the 30 year plan.*

That's about right, I am putting money away in my 401K for retirement and saving for the things I want as I go. Starting a new business would probably put that on hold. However, if I can build a self-sustaining business in three to five years that would get me there 25 years faster! So from my perspective this is a no-brainer!

*Wow, that is definitely shows me you've been listening. So your goal isn't really building a new training platform, it's to create a self-sustaining business.*

*Yup, the online training is just the vehicle to get me there.*

*I am very impressed. What do you think about what Brandy said just now, Chris and Ann?*

We're envious! I wish we would have known about the five stages of small business growth 15 years ago when we started our business. I don't think that we'd be stuck where we are now, between foundation and survival. But now we're focused on becoming self-sustainable in the next three to five years. Knowing how to avoid shiny object syndrome will help us get there faster!

*Maybe all of you can go fishing on Mike's boat in a few years!*

## What do you focus on in the maturity stage?

Why did I spent so much time on what happens in the maturity stage and not on what to do when you get here? Because when you get to maturity, you will already know what to do!

You've done it all before in the earlier stages of the growth model. Similar to the instructions you see on shampoo bottles, when you get to maturity, you continue to grow by using the small business growth model to "rinse and repeat" your way to success. Only this time, compared to when you started your business, you will have what you need to grow your new markets, products, or services, and to do it faster.

## Chapter 14: Now What Do You Do to Grow Your Business?

So you've learned a lot to this point. You know the five stages of business growth and the eight (four leadership and four management) factors that influence business growth. Next, you went through each of the stages in-depth, and learned how your area of focus for the eight factors changes within each stage. But the real test is applying what you've learned — right?

So let me take you through a quick and simple rundown to see if you're a candidate for applying the *Small Business Growth Simplified model to your business*. Just remember, simple makes it easier to see where effort is needed; simple is not a substitute for effort.

### Understanding what you read

First, you want to make sure that you understand what you've read. You probably found certain areas of the book that resonated with you. It may have been because it sounded like your situation or you may have just learned something that you didn't know before.

While it's good you got value from what you read, don't mistake understanding for diagnoses and actions. Remember this is a process. That means that it's a recipe for successful growth. If you don't follow a recipe, then the food doesn't turn out the way it's supposed to.

It's the same way with the growth model. To achieve a particular stage, you have to follow the recipe for that stage.

### Where are you and your business — really?

*Chris and Ann, do you remember the earlier discussion "At What Stage Are You and Your Business?" You found out about the Small Business Growth Questionnaire, a tool to objectively assess which stage of the model you are in. After completing the questionnaire, what did you find out about your business or yourselves that you didn't know before?*

One problem we have is that we are working on things that don't matter right now. We need to begin formalizing the things that we do so we can hire and train others as we grow the business.

*Based on your being in the survival stage, I would agree with you. That is a big part of what you need to focus on.*

Also, we need to begin really tracking where our business is coming from. That is, what marketing campaigns that we're doing. We want to increase the good ones and eliminate the ones that don't work.

*Perfect. Too many business owners think business growth is all focused on the top line and forget about all the other stuff. As a result, when problems arise, they get caught off guard and have to put out all the fires they created by focusing on the top line sales numbers and paying little or no attention to other parts of their businesses.*

*While growing sales is a must for business growth, it's not the only thing. You need to build all aspects of your business to support the growing sales or the top-line growth will stop at some point. Or even worse, you'll keep growing too much, not be able to deliver on the sales, and then see your business crash.*

*So make sure you really know where you and your business are at before your plan your next steps.*

## Working your strengths and weaknesses

*How about you Mike, what is your big take away from all this?*

Well, the assessment report showed where our strengths and weaknesses are. We're doing a lot of things right. I just need to get out of the way and give someone else the reins.

*You got all that from the report?*

Well, not entirely; talking with the group was helpful, too. Having both made it easier to see where I had a big blind spot. Now I can fix the issue and the business will be better as a result.

*Good point that you bring up about the group. I have found that using a peer group is a great tool because you can all help each other. Sometimes the problem in getting these groups going is how do you facilitate them? Using this book to guide a peer group is a great way to start. Once the group is up and running, your meeting topics can be about ways to help each other get unstuck.*

## Getting the right help

This book is meant to help you understand what to focus on in marketing, sales, and operations based on the level of maturity of your business. When you know your stage and what to focus on, then you need only a handful of strategies to get unstuck and that, in turn, makes easier to know the kind of help you need.

*For Ann and Chris's situation — do you two have a better idea of what you need?*

We don't really need a big comprehensive marketing plan and set of campaigns to achieve our next level of success. We just need to be more consistent with what gave us success in the past.

As we move forward into new residential markets, that is a whole different animal. But for now, we see the kind of success this simple approach gives us.

*What kind of results are you seeing so far from this approach?*

Well, revenue has increased by more than 52% over last year. We have had to focus our resources on preparing the operation to scale more quickly and have hired three new people in just six months. We're ready to add more technicians, and we're confident that we can do it rapidly because of what we've learned and applied so far.

*Good point. You're mastering the skills you need for your current stage, and that you'll need to keep applying to grow your business.*

## Build your business plan and your action plans!

To this point everything in the process has given you the information that you need to make better decisions. With this information and a handful of decisions, you can begin mapping out your business plan and 90-day action plans. Your business plan is your goal-post for achieving a self-sustaining business, and every 90-day action plan is a task list for systematically moving you closer to your goal.

Your business plan doesn't have to be big. In fact, our high-impact business plans are only two or three pages. If your plan is bigger than that, then you'll never look at it. You want to review it weekly, but no less than once a month.

Similarly, your 90-day action plans should be short task lists that help you stay focused on reaching objectives that are relevant to your current stage of business growth. For example, if you are stuck in survival, what objectives do you need to focus on to get unstuck? What tasks do you and your team need to complete? Write down and delegate those tasks to the people you've trained and who know they are accountable! When you review your plan weekly or at least once a month, then people will complete their tasks and your plan moves forward on its own.

For an example of a high-impact business plan and a 90-day action plan, see appendices C and D. These tools are part of our High-Impact Business Planning program. You can find this in an online training format via our website if you'd like help applying this process to your business planning.

## Monitoring as you move up the growth model

So you have assessed where you are on the growth model. You've read the parts of the book that correspond to your current stage of growth and you understand what you need to focus on next. You built your business plan and assigned tasks from your 90-day action plan.

So what's next? Monitoring your progress and adjusting your plans only as necessary!

I recommend that you hold yourself accountable by holding weekly progress-review meetings that keep others accountable. When you do, you'll quickly realize how much easier to see what's been done, and what needs to be done next in the next 90 – 120 days.

## A final discussion with our owners

*Ok, so if you had a business plan and a 90-day action plan, where do you think that you'd be Brandy?*

Well, if I had this all listed out I would hope that I'd have all my startup stuff behind me and be looking for clients. Once I had paying clients, I could focus on breaking even so I could get out of the foundation stage!

*Don't get too far ahead of yourself here. But you're right. It's possible if you focus on the things that you need to achieve that goal.*

*How about you, Ann and Chris?*

We are firmly in the survival stage and we know our strengths and weaknesses. We've updated our business plan to reflect our new goal — self-sustainability — and we have our 90-day action plan to keep us moving. Everyone has their assigned tasks and we are having weekly reviews to make sure the tasks are being completed.

We figure that we will have systems in place with a management team in the next 12 – 18 months. At that point we're pretty much in the self-sustainability stage as long as we train our successor.

*Wow, it seems a little aggressive. Are you sure you can get there?*

Absolutely, our successor is already in the door. We are training him to manage the commercial division now. So that critical success factor is already being worked.

*Well then you've got it under control. How about you Mike?*

I see how this works. I just need to spend some time lining up all my key executives and determine which ones are best suited to take over. Then I need to have them help me create a transition plan to put my successor in place and get me untangled from the day-to-day altogether.

*I like all of your plans. Just write the goals and tasks, then delegate, review, and complete the tasks, and then repeat! Now that you are focused on the right objectives you can see how quickly you can accomplish what's necessary to grow the business to the next stage.*

*Using this approach any of you can easily step away from your business in three to five years. You just need to get focused on the things you need to focus on for your stage of business growth. Complete those objectives and then move on to the next growth stage's set of objectives.*

*Mike, in your case, it might be six to twelve months or even less if everyone buys-in.*

I see that, and that's what I am hoping for.

*What you decide when you get to the self-sustainability stage is entirely up to you. But by getting there, you have a choice!*

*Most small business owners currently don't have a choice. However, if they would just follow the simple approach offered in this book, their dreams of **financial freedom**, and more importantly **life independence** are possible. So go get it and good luck!*

# Appendix A: Small Business Growth Assessment Questionnaire

## Step 1 - Complete the questionnaire

1. Answer each questions with YES or NO and provide additional information as requested.

2. Add up your number of Yes's and enter the total at the end of the questionnaire

| # | Questions | Yes/No |
|---|---|---|
| 1 | Has your business reached breakeven every month for 9 months or annually 2 consecutive years? | |
| 2 | Did you originally fund your business? If no, from where did the money come? | |
| 3 | Do you currently have employees? If yes, how many people do you currently employ? | |
| 4 | Do you require equipment to produce the product/service your business delivers? | |
| 5 | When you began your business was your primary goal something other than making money? | |
| 6 | Do you have a % profit requirement which you try to achieve each month? If yes, what %? | |
| 7 | Has your business been profitable for 9 consecutive months or annually 2 consecutive years? | |
| 8 | Do you have experience selling in the market that you serve before starting this business? How many years? | |
| 9 | Do you have prior experience with the product/service your business delivers before starting this business? How many years? | |
| 10 | Did you have profit and loss responsibility in a previous job before starting this business? | |
| 11 | Do you have written policies, procedures, and training to produce your product/service? | |
| 12 | Do you manage to a target % for your cost of goods sold (COGS) and overhead? If so, what are they? | |
| 13 | Do you retain an accountant? | |
| 14 | Do you retain a business lawyer? | |
| 15 | Do you have a business banker? | |
| 16 | Do you have a business insurance agent? | |
| 17 | Do you have a succession plan? | |

| # | Questions | Yes/No |
|---|-----------|--------|
| 18 | If you have a succession plan, is the person that will fill your role identified and being trained at this moment? | |
| 19 | Do you have an exit strategy once you reach the goal set when you started your business? | |
| 20 | Do you know exactly how many closed sales you need to make each month to break even? | |
| 21 | Is your close rate documented and communicated throughout the company? | |
| 22 | Do you know exactly how many sales are needed each month to hit your target % profit? | |
| 23 | Is there a written sales plan for reaching the profit target and is it communicated to the sales team? | |
| 24 | Do you know what business function is your limiting factor? | |
| 25 | Do you know how much capital is needed to add capacity when you reach your limiting factor? | |
| 26 | Do you already have a source for capital when you your reach that limit? | |
| 27 | Does each employee you employ have a written job description? | |
| 28 | Do you have a method of measuring the performance of each employee? | |
| 29 | Does your employee performance tie directly to your business plan? | |
| 30 | Do you have written training/development plans for each employee? | |
| 31 | Do you have a management team? | |
| 32 | Do you conduct regularly scheduled status meetings with the management team? | |
| 33 | What is the frequency of your management meetings: Daily, Weekly, Monthly, or As Needed? | |
| 34 | Does a written accounting system exist for creating proposals/quotes, ordering materials, communicating production orders, billing customers, etc.? | |
| 35 | Do you have a written or automated method of tracking all clients, prospects, and sales in process? | |
| 36 | Do you have company assets that are tracked and show up on your balance sheet? | |
| 37 | Is your product or service unique?  If yes, do you have a patent or copyright filed to protect it? | |
| | **Overall Total** | |

## Step 2: Find your growth stage

Use the table below to determine your current stage of growth.

| Item | Your Answer | Overall Total | Then your business is ... |
|---|---|---|---|
| Question #1 | No | — | in the foundation stage |
| | YES | less than 5 | in the foundation stage |
| Questions #1 and #6 | YES | 6 – 14 | transitioning to survival stage |
| | YES | 15 – 25 | securely in survival stage (stuck in nowhere land) |
| Questions #6 and #18 | YES | 26 – 36 | transitioning to self-sustainability stage |
| Overall Total | — | 37 | securely in self-sustainability stage |

Get a more comprehensive assessment including all strengths and weaknesses in the eight growth factors using our full Small Business Growth Assessment at www.dinoeliadis.com/get-started-assessing-your-growth-stage. See an example report in the section that follows.

# Appendix B: Business Growth Assessment Executive Report

When used in conjunction with the Small Business Growth Matrix, this report is intended to guide owners in focusing resources on the right objectives to accelerate business growth and self-sustainability.

## Small Business Growth Assessment

Executive Report

# Table of Contents

Dino Eliadis, Inc.
117 N. Florida Avenue
Tarpon Springs, Florida 34689
Phone 727-487-5435• Fax 727-213-6234

# Executive Summary

Your Overall Growth Score is = 13

### Transitioning to Survival Stage - Score = 4 - 13

Based on your score you are in transition from the foundation stage to the survival stage. This means that you need to focus on getting monthly cash flow to consistent breakeven, while planning for the next goal

**Consistently achieve owner-established profit requirement.**

Use the Small Business Growth Matrix to better understand the dynamics of the foundation stage and the survival stage of the growth cycle. It will help you outline the following to achieve the next step of growth your business

- + objectives
- + challenges
- + risks
- + personal requirements
- + company requirements

Use the Small Business Growth Factor and Score by Business Function charts to see where you need to focus. Prioritize your action plan based on where both you and your company need the most help. You can use the High Impact Business Planning tool and training to assist with building your action plan.

Additionally, your strengths analysis shows you where you have assets and resources that you can leverage to achieve the goal and objectives. The weakness analysis provides a deeper look into where you need to concentrate your focus to achieve the goal and objectives of the foundation and survival stages.

If you need further assistance contact DE, Inc. We can provide you with coaching or consulting assistance in moving your business to the next stage of growth.

# Business Growth Charts

| Growth Stages | Your Score | Max Possible | Growth Factors | Your Score | Max Possible | Business Functions | Your Score | Max Possible |
|---|---|---|---|---|---|---|---|---|
| 1-Foundation | 5 | 5 | **Owner** | **4** | **19** | Admin | 4 | 10 |
| 2-Survival | 3 | 11 | Goals | 1 | 2 | Exec | 1 | 8 |
| 3-Self-Sustainability | 5 | 21 | Operational Skill | 2 | 5 | Financial | 2 | 4 |
| **Grand Total** | **13** | **37** | Managerial | 1 | 7 | HR | 2 | 6 |
| | | | Strategy | 0 | 5 | Ops | 2 | 3 |
| | | | **Company** | **9** | **18** | Sales | 2 | 6 |
| | | | Financial | 2 | 4 | **Grand Total** | **13** | **37** |
| | | | Personnel | 2 | 3 | | | |
| | | | Systems | 2 | 7 | | | |
| | | | Business Asset | 3 | 4 | | | |
| | | | **Grand Total** | **13** | **37** | | | |

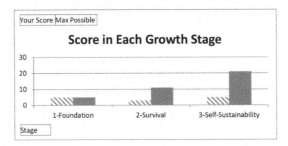

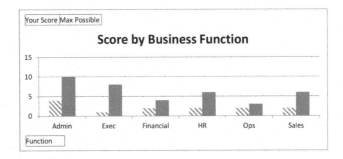

# Business Growth Strengths

Score

**Strengths**

**Owner**

### Admin

*Do you retain an accountant?*

- You are a good leader and understand the important of a tax and financial adviser for the business. Share your long-range business objectives so they can best advise you.

### Exec

*When you began your business, was your primary goal something other than making money? If yes, what was*

- Your passion for something other than money will help you achieve things others believe to be impossible.

### Ops

*Did you have experience with the product/service your business delivers before starting your business? How*

- A good understanding of how your product is built or service is delivered gives you an operational advantage which is an asset to your business.

### Sales

*Did you have experience selling in the market that you serve before starting your business? How many years?*

- Having a good understanding of your market and/or industry allows you to ramp up sales more quickly.

**Company**

### Admin

*Do you have company assets that are tracked and show up on your balance sheet?*

- Understanding the tangible things that give value to your business are critical. You may want to add intangible items to your accounting as they can give even greater value. Check with your accountant to understand how intangible assets can be used more effectively or contact DE, Inc. for more information.

*Do you conduct regularly scheduled progress meetings with the management team?*

- Management meetings shows your desire to establish accountability within your company and that it starts by holding yourself accountable.

*What is the frequency of your management meetings: daily, weekly, monthly, or as-needed?*

- You show great management skill with your understanding of the need for regular status meetings.

### Financial

*Has your business reached breakeven every month for 9 months or annually for 2 consecutive years?*

- If you've demonstrated consistent breakeven you've already achieved the first goal of the business growth model. Congratulations!

*Did you originally fund your business by yourself?*

*If not, then list all of your funding sources:*

- By showing your financial commitment to your business, it is often easier to find money later when you

### HR

*Do you have employees? If yes, how many people do you currently employ?*

- Hiring is a big step in growing your business and shows personal growth as a business owner.

*Do you have a written accounting system for creating proposals/quotes, ordering materials, communicating production orders, billing customers, and so on?*

- SOP's added to the value of your business and its ability to grow.

### Ops

*Do you require equipment to produce the product/service your business delivers?*

- You understand an importance of assets to the value of your business.

### Sales

*Do you have a written or automated method of tracking all clients, prospects, and sales in process?*

- By tracking the sales process you understand the value of intangible asset and customer service for your

# Business Growth Weaknesses

Score

| Weaknesses |
| --- |
| Owner |

### Admin

*Do you have a management team?*
- Without a management team your business can never achieve the self-sustainability stage. You must set an objective for adding and developing a management team or your business will never reach your true potential and value for life independence and financial freedom..

*Do you know what business function is your limiting factor?*
- If you don't know where your business will break next, then you are waiting for a fire to breakout. Contact DE, Inc. for a Revenue Engine Performance Checkup to determine where chokepoints exist.

*Do you have a business banker?*
- Every business needs an adviser that provides funding input and guidance for the business. Get one

*Do you have a business insurance agent?*
- Every business needs an adviser that provides risk mitigation input and guidance for the business. Get

*Do you retain a business lawyer?*
- Every business needs an adviser that provides legal input and guidance for the business. Get one

### Exec

*Do you have a % profit requirement which you try to achieve each month? If yes, what %?*
- Just being profitable each month doesn't mean your business is successful. It needs to meet your profitability requirement as an owner. If the business doesn't then you need to ask yourself "why

*Did you have profit and loss responsibility in a previous job before starting your business?*
- Not having a good foundation of financial management means learning basic financial management needs to be a personal objective.

*Do you have a succession plan?*
- Not planning for how your business will continue without you is a huge risk to your family and the family of your employees and vendors. If you don't have a succession plan speak to a trusted adviser immediately and add an objective to your business plan to work toward business succession.

*If you have a succession plan, have you identified the person who will fill your role and are you training*
- If your successor is not identified you need to make sure that all the pieces to identify and hire that person are at least documented and you are working on the timeline to make it happen.

*Do you have an exit strategy once you reach the goal you set when you started your business?*
- Your exit strategy is a major component in how you will build your business. Not having an exit strategy puts you 3 - 5 year behind when you decide to exist your business.

### Financial

*Do you know how much capital is needed to add capacity when that business function has reached its*
- Not understanding the cost to add capacity will cause you financial challenges when you need expand operations of your growing business.

### HR

*Do you have a method of measuring the performance of each employee?*
- Without a good performance evaluation system your business is not operating optimally. You may even be experiencing high turnover and poor employee performance.

*Does each employee have a written job description?*
- Without job descriptions your company is at risk for employment suits and hire/fire challenges. Additionally, your business' accountability is questionable.

### Sales

*Is your close rate documented and communicated throughout the company?*
- Even if you know your close rate everyone must know it or the entire team is not focused on the sales objective. Remember everyone sells and everyone services in a successful business.

*Do you have a written sales plan for reaching your profit target and does your sales team know it?*
- If you don't have a sales plan then you've not created accountability in achieving the company revenue goal. Meeting your profit requirement starts by achieving your revenue goal, so manage it!

### Company

### Admin

*Do you have written training/development plans for each employee?*
- You will gain greater employee productivity if they feel that you care about their career progression. Determine how you can make this part of your HR system.

### Exec

*Has your business been profitable for 9 consecutive months or annually for 2 consecutive years?*
- Consistent profitability is the only goal of the survival stage. If you cannot consistently achieve your profit requirement each month this should be the only goal of your business plan until you achieve it.

*Is your product or service unique? If yes, do you have a patent, trademark, or copyright filed to protect it?*
- not protecting your intellectual property can decrease the value of your business or Even worse put you out of business If someone patents or copyrights part of your offerings.

### Financial

*Do you manage to a target % for your cost of goods sold (COGS) and overhead? If so, what is the target*
- Without financial metrics it is nearly impossible to manage the financial health of your business. Determine these % for your business as soon as possible. Then use them to manage company

### HR

*Does your employee performance tie directly to your business plan?*
- No or a generic employee evaluation system usually do not allow for optimum performance within the organization and can lead to legal challenges during dismissal situations.

*Do you already have a source for capital when you reach that limit?*
- If you do not have a funding source set an objective to find one so that this doesn't become an obstacle in the middle of expanding your business. Companies in this scenario go bankrupt all the

### Ops

*Do you have written policies, procedures, and training to produce your product/service?*
- Without standard operating procedures (SOP's) it is difficult to expand and assure consistent quality. These are critical factors in building market value.

### Sales

*Do you know exactly how many closed sales you need to make each month to break even?*
- Knowing your "close rate" is a critical metric of tuning your revenue engine. If you don't know your "close rate" you should learn how to calculate it immediately.

*Do you know exactly how many sales are needed each month to hit your target % profit?*
- Not understanding how many sales you need to hit your sales target means you're not forecasting your sales and leaving the fate of your company to chance. Figure how many sales you need to hit

# Appendix C: High-Impact Business Plan — Example

## Business Plan
For
## Excellence Carpet Cleaning

### Vision Statement:
Grow a self-sustaining business focused on developing stronger employee relationships that helps create better leaders for their families while increasing total annual revenue to $400,000 averaging 30% net profit.

### *Keys to Success:*
The following are key factors that will impact the success in achieving the vision for this business:

- ✓ Establish benchmarks and minimum requirements for all aspects of the business including customer service, marketing/sales, service delivery, financial management, and administration.
- • Establish sound hiring practices so that the right kind of people are hired to support the vision.
- • Have a greater focus on new customer acquisition that grows the base for repeat residential customers.
- • Develop marketing and sales systems that are repeatable and scalable that allow Excellence Carpet Cleaning (ECC) to transition into residential market.
- ✓ Establish better reporting systems that allow for better management and accountability across the company and improves communication.

### This Year's Business Goal:
Achieve $250,000 ($175k-comm, $75k res) in revenue while creating the foundational support system to support growth of residential sector of the market of the business' vision.

### *Business Objectives:*
The following set of objective are required to support achieving the annual goal:

- • Develop a sales & marketing plan to sustain job volume to support the monthly revenue goal of $14,500 per month in support of the business goal.
- • Develop a sales and marketing plan to grow the residential side of the business with the monthly goal of $6500.
- • Outline a company code of ethics and begin establishing methods of their delivery via Excellence Carpet Cleaning policies & procedures.
- • Begin a policy & procedure for critical functions where hires will be made first to establish performance standards and accountability.
- • Implement customer service standard by which the Excellence Carpet Cleaning mission is delivered by its employees.

## Functional goals & Objectives:

This section outlines the goals and objectives required department by department to achieve annual goal:

### Marketing:

Goal: Develop a marketing plan for residential market to reach goal of $6,500/month in sales.

Marketing Objectives:
- Develop residential marketing strategy (website, referral, etc.)
- Put measures in place to track the different campaigns

### Sales:

Goal: Work sales plan to achieve $175,000 in commercial sales and $75,000 in residential sales.

Sales Objectives:
- Get more familiar with CRM systems and it's reporting.
- Create regular calling plan for targeted commercial properties.
- Develop and implement sales campaign for short-fall months (i.e. discount prices A/C drain clearing).
- Begin collecting data and information about how to sell and market to residential customers.

### Operations:

Goal: Get all our services documented so that they can more quickly support growth for the company.

Operational Objectives:
- Get anything already written into an editable document
- Document all our services and get standardize training plan established for new techs.
- Develop a capital budget necessary to bring on a new tech with completely outfitted a truck with equipment and necessary supplies.

### Accounting & Finance:

Goal: Establish regular reporting including setting up and conducting regular monthly owner meetings.

Operational Objectives:
- Create and document schedule for weekly entering (invoices, receipts, checks, deposits, statements).
- Better monitor A/R and A/P to assure growth does not put company into a negative financial position.
- Establish a line of credit to help with cash flow issue as business grows.

### Administration:

Goal: Finalize policy and procedure manual

Operational Objectives:
- Establish standardized hiring process and needed support materials to support more hires.
- Develop better communication tools to handle higher volume of work from field with growth
- Implement service system to better monitor and manage jobs, work orders, and employee timecards.

# Appendix D: 90-Day Action Plan — Example

## ECC 2nd Quarter Action Plan

### Goal:
1. Determine best marketing results to continue growth in the residential market.
2. Create Capitol Budget for new truck and cleaning equipment

### Objectives:
- ∞ Develop residential marketing strategy
- ∞ Create regular calling plan for targeted commercial properties
- ∞ Develop and implement sales campaign for short-fall months (discounting prices on items like A/C Drain clearing)
- ∞ Begin collecting data and information about how to sell and market to residential customers
- ∞ Vehicle maintenance and finalize 3rd van set-up

### Resources:

| | | |
|---|---|---|
| vehicle maintenance records | Website | Service sales sheet |
| ECC annual budget | Past publication adverts | Online review sites |
| | | |

### Action Plan:

| Activities | Planned Complete | Actual Complete |
|---|---|---|
| 1. Join Chamber and set up chamber contact page (create new service listing page? Find most popular terms-Google Ad Words) | 5/15/15 | |
| 2. Outline Repair vs Replace campaign | 6/30/15 | |
| 3. Develop hair salon contact protocol | 5/29/15 | |
| 4. Visit hair salons signed up with Chamber | 6/30/15 | |
| 5. Create Service/Products email to send out to current properties | 5/29/15 | |
| 6. Have Chamber ad pay and ready to send over | 6/8/15 | |
| 7. Testimonials as to why they switched to us | 5/22/15 | |
| 8. Get answers to the 3 questions for apartments | 5/22/15 | |
| 9. Create list of services and campaign for short-fall months to help compensate | 6/30/15 | |
| 10. Create Capitol Budget-how much to get a tuck/machine/employee | 5/29/15 | |
| 11. Replace transmission in 2008 Chevy | 5/29/15 | |
| 12. | | |

# Appendix E: Business Growth Resources

### Small Business Growth Assessment
The Small Business Growth Assessment helps you determine your
current growth stage and pinpoint what weaknesses you need to improve
and which strengths you can use to accelerate your business to the next
growth stage.

http://dinoeliadis.com/get-started-assessing-your-growth-stage/

### Tuning Your Revenue Engine
The revenue engine is a metaphor DE, Inc. created to simplify the
understanding of business management so you understand the
operational causes that effect your financials so you can predictively
improve your cash flow.

http://dinoeliadis.com/business-growth/small-business-management

### Strategic Planning and Recovery Cycle (SPARC)
SPARC consists of six steps. Three steps help you focus and prioritize
strategically. Three steps are intended to help you focus and prioritize
resources tactically to execute to achieve your desired outcome.

http://dinoeliadis.com/business-solution

### High Impact Business Planning
A business plan should be helpful not hindering! This business tool
focuses everything helps you organize your day-to-day operation to meet
your annual business goal and objectives into a 3 page plan with a 1 page
budget. Use quarterly action plans help you delegate and create
accountability across your business.

http://dinoeliadis.com/business-planning-with-high-impact